THE NO- WHEAT COOKBOOK

Easy, delicious recipes for a wheat-free diet

Series Editor, Kimberly A. Tessmer, RD, LD

A **adams**media
Avon, Massachusetts

Published by
Adams Media, a division of F+W Media, Inc.
57 Littlefield Street, Avon, MA 02322. U.S.A.
www.adamsmedia.com

Contains material adapted and abridged from *The Everything® Wheat-Free Diet Cookbook* by Lauren Kelly, copyright © 2013 by F+W Media, Inc., ISBN-10: 1-4405-5680-6, ISBN-13: 978-1-4405-5680-7; and *The No-Gluten Cookbook* by Kimberly A. Tessmer, RD, LD, copyright © 2007 by F+W Media, Inc., ISBN-10: 1-59869-089-2, ISBN-13: 978-1-59869-089-7.

ISBN 10: 1-4405-6745-X
ISBN 13: 978-1-4405-6745-2
eISBN 10: 1-4405-6746-8
eISBN 13: 978-1-4405-6746-9

Printed in the United States of America.

10 9 8 7 6 5 4 3 2 1

This book is available at quantity discounts for bulk purchases.
For information, please call 1-800-289-0963.

Dedication

I dedicate this wonderful collection of wheat-free recipes to all the people who must diligently work each day to ensure they are eliminating wheat from their diet. I hope that these recipes will make life a bit easier and a lot tastier. I also dedicate this cookbook to both my late mom, Nancy Bradford, and my late father-in-law, Fred Tessmer, who both loved to cook and were great at it!

Acknowledgments

Thanks to the team at Adams Media, especially Ross Weisman for all his help with this project.

Introduction

We normally hear that wheat is good for us. So why would you need a wheat-free cookbook? That sounds like a fair question, doesn't it? Dietitians have educated us on how important it is to consume a well-balanced diet. Over the last decade we have been informed how crucial it is to incorporate more whole grains and wheat into our daily lives as part of a healthy well-balanced diet. Whole wheat most definitely contains vital complex carbohydrates, dietary fiber, antioxidants, vitamins, and minerals, but unfortunately some people are not able to take advantage of these many nutritional perks. There are many people that have an allergy and/or intolerance to wheat. In fact, a wheat allergy is one of the most common food allergies in children. Although allergies are not the only reason some people go wheat-free, it is one of the main reasons.

Treatment for wheat allergies is avoiding all wheat. This sounds simple, but it can be a difficult adjustment to your daily diet. Wheat is a main ingredient in many foods including breads, pasta, cakes, crackers, cookies, cereals, beer, condiments—the list goes on. It can be an obvious ingredient in some foods and a hidden ingredient in others. Sometimes just a visit to a restaurant, a friend's house, and even your own kitchen can prove hazardous to the uninformed. Each ingredient list and food label must continually and thoroughly be inspected, and a well-thought-out approach must be initiated to safeguard against foods containing wheat.

It is hoped that this book will demonstrate that you don't have to make drastic changes to your lifestyle to eat a wheat-free diet once you know and understand the facts. For instance, there are many alternative ingredients to wheat flour including corn, rice, almond, and even coconut—just to name a few—that allow you to still prepare breads, cakes, cookies, and other favorite foods. These alternative flours will make your meals taste just as delicious without noticing the difference. And just as there are alternatives to wheat flour, there are tasty alternatives to many other food products that contain wheat.

Though it is vital to be thoroughly educated by a nutritional professional, such as a registered dietitian, as you begin your wheat-free diet, this cookbook can be a great additional resource to help you get started with a variety of delicious meals, soups, desserts, and snacks that you and your family will enjoy!

Important Note: Many foods within this cookbook are marked "wheat-free." The ingredients of these foods must be analyzed by brand to ensure they are wheat-free. All companies create different versions of different foods, so you must check food labels carefully and never assume that a food is wheat-free. It is a smart idea to get in the habit of checking *all* foods, whether you know they are wheat-free or not, including those within each recipe of this book.

The Basis of a
Wheat-Free Diet

Chapter 1

As you begin a wheat-free diet, you may feel discouraged and severely restricted in what you can and can't eat. Adjusting to a wheat-free diet doesn't have to be as overwhelming as you might think. With the public's growing awareness that food allergies are on the rise, ingredients supporting a wheat-free lifestyle are now becoming easier to find. Visit your favorite supermarket or specialty store and you're sure to find loads of alternatives to wheat. There are also many websites that cater to those with food allergies and that carry specialty ingredients and food products. With proper education from a healthcare professional such as a registered dietitian and a little research and experimentation, you'll discover it can actually be fun and easy to cook delicious, healthy, wheat-free meals for the whole family.

Living Wheat-Free

It can be normal to feel overwhelmed when you are told that you need to follow a wheat-free diet. Many of your concerns and questions are legitimate. You may be asking, Will I need to radically change my lifestyle? What will I be able to eat? Will I have to sacrifice flavor and foods that I love? What will I feed my family? There is no question that you will need to alter your lifestyle in some ways and that you will need to eliminate all wheat from your diet. However, the changes don't need to be as radical as you might expect, and you will be able to manage your new lifestyle, and eventually, even come to embrace it. And don't worry, there is no need to sacrifice your favorite delicious meals—there are many substitutions for wheat that will make your meals taste like you have always remembered them.

Common Food Allergies

Wheat is one of the eight most common food allergies, along with peanuts, tree nuts (walnuts, cashews, pecans, almonds, Brazil nuts, macadamia nuts, chestnuts, pine nuts, and pistachios), fish, shellfish, eggs, milk, and soy.

There are some people who must medically follow a wheat-free diet due to a severe allergy or an intolerance. However there are also people of all ages and from all walks of life that choose to live wheat-free. Some studies have shown that wheat may cause inflammation in the body for some people, which can lead to several chronic illnesses, so many people give up wheat in order to help reduce inflammation and feel better.

The Difference Between a Wheat Allergy and Celiac Disease

Wheat allergies can sometimes be confused with celiac disease. Although there are a few similarities, these two conditions are very different disorders with very different treatments. Celiac disease is an autoimmune disorder in which one particular protein found in wheat, called gluten, causes an abnormal immune system response within the small intestine. It affects one out of every 133 people in the United States and is a lifelong condition. There is no cure for celiac disease and the only treatment is a strict 100 percent gluten-free diet. Gluten is not only found in wheat but in barley and rye as well. Gluten is the part of flour that gives dough its structure and leavening abilities. Gluten can be found in a wide variety of foods including baked goods (such as breads, cookies, and cakes), pasta, cereals, sauces, soups, seasonings, candy, preservatives, and even some medications.

For people with celiac disease, consuming any amount of gluten will set off an autoimmune response that causes the destruction of the villi within the lining of the small intestines as well as the destruction of digestive enzymes. Their body produces antibodies that attack the small intestines, causing damage, debilitating symptoms, and illness. The destruction of the villi results in the body's inability to absorb nutrients that are needed for good health such as carbohydrates, protein, and fat, as well as essential vitamins and minerals. In turn these nutritional deficiencies can deprive the brain, nervous system, bones, liver, heart, and other organs of the nourishment they need and cause many types of serious health issues and illnesses. People with celiac disease can suffer with a host of symptoms, and it varies greatly from individual to individual. Symptoms can include but are not limited to recurring abdominal bloating and pain, nausea, vomiting, diarrhea, weight loss, iron deficiency anemia, nutritional deficiencies, edema, excessive gas, chronic fatigue, weakness, depression, bone or joint pain, muscle cramps, constipation, balance problems, migraine headaches, seizures, memory issues, dental defects, infertility, and failure to thrive in children. As stated above, there is no cure for celiac disease. It is a permanent reaction to gluten, and individuals with the disease must completely avoid any foods containing wheat, barley, or rye for life.

A person should never follow a gluten-free diet before they have been properly diagnosed. This can interfere with test results and therefore a correct diagnosis.

A wheat allergy is much different than what was described for celiac disease. A wheat allergy is described as generating an allergy-causing antibody to proteins found in wheat. In a wheat allergy, there are four different classes of proteins (in wheat) that can cause an allergic reaction: gluten, albumin, globulin, and gliadin. People with wheat allergies do not experience the same problems with absorption and damage to the small intestines as someone with celiac disease. Instead, when a person with a wheat allergy consumes wheat (and that includes wheat only), they experience a one-time allergic reaction that does not continue to do damage as in celiac disease. When a person with a wheat allergy consumes wheat, they will most likely experience a reaction within a few minutes to a few hours. Some people may have a slight sensitivity to wheat, which causes some mild discomfort, while others may experience more severe reactions. Reactions can include swelling and/or itching of the mouth and/or throat; hives; nasal congestion; itchy and watery eyes; breathing difficulties; cramps, nausea and/or vomiting; diarrhea; and/or anaphylaxis, which can be a life-threatening reaction.

Label Safety

Just because a product is labeled "gluten-free" does not guarantee that it is "wheat-free." According to *http://wheat-free.org*, some manufacturers use wheat that has the gluten removed to make gluten-free foods. Make sure to always read food labels carefully.

Wheat allergies tend to develop early in life, as in infancy or toddler years. The majority of children who have a wheat allergy also tend to suffer from other food allergies such as dairy, eggs, and/or nuts. The good news is that many of these children will outgrow their wheat allergy between the ages of three and five. Children can become extremely ill when consuming wheat or even simply when they come in contact with it. People with a severe wheat allergy must learn how to take every possible precaution in order to prevent serious reactions. The only real remedy for this allergy is to avoid wheat in its entirety. Wheat allergies seem to not be as common in adolescents and adults. If you feel you or your child may have a wheat allergy or intolerance, it is vital to visit your physician and not to self-diagnose. There are many conditions that can mimic the same symptoms as a wheat allergy or intolerance.

Food Allergies Versus Food Intolerance
The main difference between a food allergy and a food intolerance is that food allergies affect the immune system while food intolerances do not.

Wheat intolerance is much more common than wheat allergies, and those who have it usually have a delayed onset of symptoms, as long as two to three days later. These people suffer with various degrees of symptoms, ranging from stomach discomfort to chronic headaches and diarrhea.

What You Can and Can't Eat
Before beginning a wheat-free diet, always consult your doctor and a nutrition professional such as a registered dietitian to ensure a wheat-free diet is right for you and to receive the proper instruction and education. As overwhelming as it may initially seem, there are many foods that you can still eat while on a wheat-free diet. To start out, all fresh foods such as fruits, vegetables, plain meats, and some starches such as quinoa and rice are wheat-free. And there are many more options available than you may think. You may be surprised by the number of wheat-free choices available in your local grocery or specialty store. You will not be able to use white or wheat flour, but you can certainly use rice, almond, coconut, tapioca, or corn flour, just to name a few. You may not be able to eat

ready-made pancakes, but you can easily make your own wheat-free pancakes. Once you have the necessary knowledge to make the correct choices and get in the habit of always reading food labels, a wheat-free diet will become second nature for you.

Food Preparation Safety
Often, it is the way foods are prepared that poses a problem. For example, once chicken becomes breaded, it is no longer wheat-free. But you could easily use wheat-free bread crumbs and flour and still be able to enjoy this classic dish.

The most important rule for following a wheat-free diet is to read food labels and ingredient lists carefully. There are many foods out there that contain some type of wheat ingredient that might surprise you. For example, did you know that soy sauce could contain wheat? Even dairy products like ice cream and sour cream may have some wheat in them. If you are unsure of which ingredients might contain wheat, call the manufacturer. To understand how to correctly read ingredients lists for wheat products you must first be properly educated by a healthcare professional.

Ingredients with Wheat
Some common ingredients that contain wheat that you may not be aware of include: graham, bulghur, wheat germ, modified food starch, spelt, and semolina.

Even some nonfood items may contain wheat such as medications, cosmetics, glue, lotions, ointments, dog food, clays, shampoo, sunscreens, and vitamins. If your allergy is severe enough, even simply touching wheat can cause an allergic reaction. Call the manufacturer to find out if there is wheat in specific products if you are not sure.

In the Event of Contact
For those with severe wheat allergies, there are medical treatments available in the event that they come in contact with wheat. Even though a food may not be made with wheat it can still be contaminated by a food that is made with wheat and cause problems. Antihistamines, a type of

medication that helps to relieve allergy symptoms, should be taken after exposure to wheat. Individuals at risk of more serious reactions, such as anaphylaxis, must carry two doses of the emergency medication epinephrine (synthetic adrenaline) with them at all times. This medication, commonly administered in the form of an EpiPen, allows the victim to breathe better and helps restore blood pressure to normal levels.

Eating Out

If you are concerned about wheat contained in meals when you are eating out at a restaurant, do not hesitate to call beforehand and ask. Today many restaurants actually prepare and serve gluten- and wheat-free dishes. Know the obvious offenders when reading the menu at your favorite restaurant. Your first inclination must be to exclude any pasta, salad (dressings and croutons may contain wheat), marinades, sauces, and sandwiches. Anything that is deep-fried, breaded, or battered most likely contains wheat.

It's not just food you need to be concerned about on a wheat-free diet. That drink you order with your meal can be just as dangerous. Beer, ale, root beer, malted milk, and even instant chocolate drink mixes can contain wheat. After dinner, you'll also have to be careful of what type of coffee you drink as many instant coffees contain wheat. If you are in doubt, be safe and avoid it completely.

Children and the Wheat-Free Lifestyle

It can be very difficult to watch a child suffer with a food allergy. It is even harder when you don't know what the child is suffering from. Symptoms can appear in very young children, even infants, but they can't tell you what's bothering them. If you suspect your child is suffering from a food intolerance or food allergy, consult your pediatrician immediately. Once a positive diagnosis has been confirmed, you will need to modify your child's diet and lifestyle immediately. You and your child do not need to feel alone in this process. Gather support from friends, family, teachers, and classmates. You might even decide to convert the whole family to a wheat-free diet to make it easier for the child.

School Safety

Be sure to alert your child's school to the fact that your child suffers from a wheat allergy or intolerance. This will help prevent any potential exposures to wheat.

Monitoring your child's diet is much more manageable to do when he or she is at home. Once your child leaves the house, your fears and anxieties will escalate, as there is an increased chance your child could potentially come in contact with an offending food containing wheat. But you can take steps to safeguard your child against these situations. First, contact your child's school. The school nurse will be able to provide you with guidance. Next, the best way to avoid any contact with wheat is to prepare your child's lunch. Buying lunch at school is not an option. Even though something may appear to be wheat-free, you can never be 100 percent sure it wasn't contaminated by being prepared on a surface that already had wheat on it. Your child can enjoy social gatherings and birthday parties as long as the necessary precautions are taken. If your child is attending a friend's birthday party, pack your own special, wheat-free treats (cupcakes or cookies) so he/she doesn't feel left out. It is extremely important that your child not feel like an outcast because of his or her allergy. Your child will learn to adapt and eventually embrace this new lifestyle.

Wheat Dangers in Nonfood Items

You must be aware of the nonfood items that contain wheat. For instance, Play-Doh actually contains wheat. Some craft items and glues can also contain wheat. Parents need to stay informed about craft supplies that may contain wheat. There are many websites that inform parents about how to make their own wheat-free craft materials such as *www.theglutengal.com*, *www.momsplaceglutenfree.com*, and *www.kidceliac.com*.

Wheat-Free for Life

Over time, and with some creativity and patience, you will be able to enjoy a wheat-free lifestyle. Cooking and baking wheat-free meals can be quite intimidating at first. You may strike out with your first few attempts, but don't be discouraged. Continue to experiment with a wide array of ingredients, and eventually, you will be thrilled with the results.

Essential Equipment

Make sure you own a food processor or high-speed blender. These appliances come in handy while experimenting with alternative ingredients. Soon you will be creating your own delicious and healthy smoothies, salsas, and sauces. Many of these sauces will be a key staple to a lot of the dishes you prepare for your family.

One very important issue you need to consider in living the wheat-free lifestyle is cross-contamination. Wheat-free foods may come in contact with those containing wheat during the manufacturing process or even at home. Oats are a perfect example of this. Some manufacturing companies process oats in the same facility as their wheat products. Today, companies are aware of the potential for cross-contamination and are labeling their products accordingly. You need to be just as disciplined in your own kitchen. You must be vigilant about not using the same cooking utensils that may have been in contact with a food containing wheat. For instance, once you begin your wheat-free lifestyle, you will need to ensure that you clean out your toaster regularly. The crumbs from the wheat bread may come in contact with wheat-free bread, resulting in an allergic reaction when consumed. If someone has a severe wheat allergy, it is recommended to have two appliances, one dedicated solely for wheat-free. Also, if your whole family isn't following a wheat-free diet, make sure to use a clean utensil when you spread peanut butter on your wheat-free toast.

Preparing foods in advance will make your life a little easier. On the weekends, prepare some snacks and meals for the upcoming week. If you need to, freeze some for future meals. Prepare your lunch (and your children's lunches) the night before. This way you are carefully packing the next day's lunch and are fully aware of what you (or your child) are eating. Leaving a refrigerated cooler in your car with healthy, wheat-free snacks also alleviates the stress of wondering what you will be able to eat.

You don't need to feel deprived while following a wheat-free diet. You can eat wheat-free meals and desserts that are not only healthy but also delicious. Use your imagination, and remember, it may take you a few times to perfect the dish, but that's the fun part. Have fun while experimenting, read your labels carefully, and stay healthy. You will not only feel better physically, but you will also feel more confident the next time you sit at the dinner table, restaurant, or that next social gathering. Here's to many years of happy, healthy wheat-free eating!

Breakfast and Brunch

Chapter 2

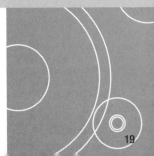

Crustless Vegetable Quiche Cups

Serves 12

1 tablespoon canola oil
½ cup finely chopped onion
1 cup fresh organic spinach
1 cup fresh grape or cherry
  tomatoes, halved
2 cups fresh mushrooms, diced
2 whole eggs, beaten
6 egg whites, beaten
1 cup Cheddar cheese
¼ teaspoon thyme
½ teaspoon sweet basil
¼ teaspoon oregano
¼ teaspoon salt
⅛ teaspoon pepper

This protein-packed breakfast can be made with whatever vegetables you have on hand. It's also the perfect way to sneak in your daily dose of vegetables.

1. Preheat the oven to 350°F. Lightly spray a 12-cup muffin tin with nonstick cooking spray or line with cupcake liners.

2. Heat oil in a large skillet over medium-high heat. Add the onions and cook, stirring occasionally, until onions are soft, about 2–3 minutes. Stir in spinach, tomatoes, and mushrooms, and continue cooking until veggies have wilted, about 3–4 minutes.

3. In a large bowl, combine the eggs, egg whites, cheese, thyme, basil, oregano, salt, and pepper. Add spinach mixture and stir to blend. Pour into prepared muffin tins.

4. Bake in preheated oven until eggs have set, about 30 minutes. Let cool for 10 minutes before serving.

Powerful Protein

Studies show that people who consume a breakfast that contains protein tend to eat less throughout the day. One quiche cup has over 6 grams of protein!

Coconut Flour Pancakes

Cooking with wheat-free flours can be intimidating, but the sweet taste of coconut flour in these pancakes proves that even wheat-free pancakes can be delicious. You can replace the coconut oil with melted butter and the coconut milk with regular milk if you prefer.

1. In a large bowl, using a wire whisk, mix together the eggs and egg whites, 3 tablespoons coconut oil, coconut milk, maple syrup, and salt.

2. Add the coconut flour and baking powder, whisking until thoroughly mixed. Add the cinnamon, allspice, flaxseed, and vanilla. Stir to combine thoroughly.

3. Heat the remaining tablespoon of coconut oil in a skillet over medium heat.

4. Spoon 2–3 tablespoons of batter onto skillet, making pancakes about 3"–4" in diameter. Cook 3–5 minutes, turning once.

Serves 3

2 whole eggs
2 egg whites
4 tablespoons coconut oil, divided
3 tablespoons coconut milk
1½ teaspoons maple syrup
1 teaspoon sea salt
3 tablespoons coconut flour
½ teaspoon wheat-free baking powder
1 teaspoon cinnamon
1 teaspoon allspice
⅓ cup ground flaxseed
1 teaspoon wheat-free vanilla extract

The Best Grain-Free Banana Bread Ever

Serves 10

¼ cup butter, softened
⅔ cup turbinado sugar
2 eggs
3 tablespoons plain nonfat Greek yogurt, wheat-free
2 tablespoons water
1 teaspoon wheat-free vanilla extract
2 tablespoons ground flaxseed
2 cups brown rice flour or rice flour
1 teaspoon wheat-free baking powder
½ teaspoon baking soda
½ teaspoon salt
½ teaspoon cinnamon
1 cup mashed ripe banana (approximately 3 large bananas)
⅓ cup finely chopped walnuts (optional)

Even those who don't need to be on a wheat-free diet will adore this banana bread. It tastes just as good with or without the walnuts.

1. Preheat the oven to 350°F.

2. In a large bowl, beat the butter and sugar until creamy. Beat in the eggs, one at a time.

3. Stir in yogurt, water, and vanilla and mix well.

4. In a separate bowl combine the flaxseed, rice flour, baking powder, baking soda, salt, and cinnamon. Add this mixture to the butter mixture.

5. Stir in the bananas and mix well. Add walnuts, if using.

6. Spoon the mixture into two or three greased mini loaf pans (5½" × 3") or one large loaf pan (5" × 10").

7. Bake 50–55 minutes, or until a wooden pick inserted into the center of the bread comes out clean.

8. Cool in the pans for 2 minutes, then turn out and cool completely.

Brown Rice Flour

Brown rice flour has more fiber and B vitamins than regular rice flour. It also offers a nutty, slightly sweet taste as opposed to regular rice flour so it may be a better alternative for cookies and baked goods.

Chestnut Flour Crepes

Chestnut flour is sweet and nutty, making the most delicious crepes you can imagine. You can stuff them with fruit and whipped cream or with your favorite wheat-free savory filling.

1. In a food processor, add the eggs, milk, and salt, and process until blended.

2. With the motor on low, slowly add the flours, stopping occasionally to scrape down the sides of the container.

3. Add the sugar if you are making sweet crepes with sweet filling; omit if you are going to fill them with savory delights.

4. Heat 1 tablespoon butter in a nonstick sauté pan over medium heat. Pour in batter by the half-cupful into the hot pan. Tilt the pan to spread the batter thinly.

5. Fry the crepes, turning, until browned, about 3–4 minutes on both sides; place on waxed paper and sprinkle with a bit of rice flour to prevent them from sticking.

6. When the crepes are done, you can fill them right away or store them in the refrigerator or freezer for later use.

Using Nonstick Sauté Pans

Nonstick pans take all of the grief out of making crepes. However, even if your pan is quite new, it's important to use a bit of butter for insurance and extra flavor. Keep the pan well buttered and you have an almost foolproof method for making perfect crepes.

Makes 12 crepes

2 eggs
1 cup milk
½ teaspoon salt
½ cup chestnut flour
½ cup rice flour
2 teaspoons sugar (optional)
2 tablespoons butter, melted
(plus more for pan)

Vegetable-Egg Scramble with Fontina Cheese

Serves 1

1 tablespoon grapeseed oil
1 clove garlic, chopped
1 cup chopped broccoli
½ cup sliced grape tomatoes
1 whole egg
2 egg whites
2 tablespoons fresh basil
½ teaspoon sea salt
1 teaspoon oregano
1 tablespoon shredded fontina
   cheese

This light dish will be your favorite way to get your daily requirements of vegetables. If you don't have broccoli or tomatoes, use whatever vegetables you have on hand.

1. Heat the oil in a medium skillet over medium-high heat. Sauté the garlic for 1 minute, then add the broccoli and tomatoes. Cook for 2–3 minutes until broccoli is tender, but still crunchy.

2. Whisk egg and egg whites in a bowl until frothy.

3. Pour eggs into skillet and continue to mix thoroughly while eggs cook. Add basil, salt, oregano, and cheese and cook for 3–4 minutes until eggs have light brown edges. Remove from heat and serve immediately.

Don't Pass on the Yolks, Folks

Are you using only egg whites? The yolks have a bad reputation, but they really are quite healthy. Yes, the yolks do contain cholesterol and fat, but moderate consumption of yolks will not put you at risk for the diseases they were once thought to have contributed to. Egg yolks provide high quality protein along with calcium and zinc, just to name a few nutrients, so don't be afraid to have some whole eggs!

Corn Crepes

You can make these crepes in advance and store them in the refrigerator or freezer.

1. Place the eggs, milk, and salt in your food processor and process until smooth.

2. With the motor on low, slowly add the flour, and spoon in the sugar (if you are making sweet crepes). Scrape down the sides of the container often. Add the melted butter.

3. Heat oil in a nonstick pan over medium heat. Pour in 1 cup batter. Tilt the pan to spread the batter evenly. Cook for 3–4 minutes, turning once. Repeat with remaining batter.

4. Place crepes on sheets of waxed paper that have been dusted with extra corn flour.

5. To store, place in a plastic bag in refrigerator or freezer. You can stuff these with wheat-free salsa, jack cheese, and sour cream, or you can stuff them with mashed fruit such as blueberries.

Storing Crepes
To store crepes, simply put a bit of corn flour on sheets of waxed paper and stack the crepes individually. Put the whole thing in a plastic bag and store in the refrigerator for up to 3 days.

Makes 12 crepes

2 eggs
1 cup milk or buttermilk
1 teaspoon salt
1 cup corn flour
2 teaspoons sugar (optional)
2 tablespoons butter, melted
1 tablespoon vegetable oil, plus
   more if needed

Shirred Eggs and Asparagus au Gratin

Serves 4

1 pound fresh asparagus, ends
trimmed, or 2 (10-ounce)
packages frozen
8 eggs
1 cup crumbled Roquefort
cheese
½ teaspoon salt
½ teaspoon pepper

This is a very easy brunch or supper dish. Fresh asparagus definitely works best in this recipe. The trick is arranging the asparagus evenly in the pan.

1. Preheat the oven to 350°F.

2. Blanch the asparagus in boiling water for 5 minutes. Take immediately out of the boiling water and place in ice water and drain.

3. Prepare a gratin pan or baking dish with nonstick spray and arrange the asparagus in the bottom in a single layer. Break the eggs over the top. Sprinkle with Roquefort, salt, and pepper, and bake until eggs are done and cheese is hot and runny (about 12 minutes). Serve hot.

Banana Pancakes

For a lighter pancake, separate the eggs and beat the whites stiffly. The bananas can be either sliced onto the cakes or mashed and incorporated into the batter.

1. In the bowl of a food processor, process all of the liquid ingredients together. Slowly add the baking powder, banana, and flour and process until smooth.

2. Heat a griddle pan or large frying pan over medium heat. Drop a teaspoon of butter on it and when the butter sizzles, start pouring on the batter to about 2" in diameter.

3. When bubbles come to the top, turn the pancakes and continue to fry until golden brown. Place on a plate in a warm oven to keep the pancakes warm while you make the others.

Flour Substitutions
Try substituting rice or potato flour in some recipes, and chickpea flour also makes an excellent savory pancake. You have so many choices—it's fun to exercise them.

Makes 16 pancakes

½ cup milk
2 eggs
1½ tablespoons butter, melted
1 tablespoon wheat-free baking powder
1 banana
1 cup rice flour (or substitute corn, chickpea, or tapioca flour)
Extra butter for frying pancakes

Egg-and-Cheese-Stuffed Tomatoes

Serves 4

8 medium tomatoes
2 cloves garlic, minced or put
 through a garlic press
4 tablespoons butter
1 teaspoon salt
1 teaspoon black pepper
1 teaspoon dried oregano
1 teaspoon cumin powder
8 eggs
½ cup grated Monterey jack or
 Cheddar cheese
8 teaspoons wheat-free corn
 bread crumbs

These are simple but look sophisticated. Their presentation is pretty and is perfect for a brunch with friends and family.

1. Cut the tops off the tomatoes, core, and using a melon baller, scoop out seeds and pulp. Place the tomatoes on a baking sheet covered with parchment paper or sprayed with nonstick spray.

2. Preheat the oven to 350°F.

3. In a skillet over medium heat, sauté the garlic in the butter for 2 minutes.

4. In a small bowl, mix together the salt, black pepper, oregano, and cumin. Spread ½ of the mixture on the insides of the tomatoes, saving the rest for topping.

5. Spoon the butter and garlic mixture into the tomatoes. Sprinkle with ½ of the remaining spice mixture.

6. Break an egg into each tomato. Sprinkle with the rest of the spice mixture.

7. Loosely spoon the cheese over the eggs, then sprinkle 1 teaspoon of the corn bread crumbs over each tomato.

8. Bake for 20 minutes. The tomatoes should still be firm, the eggs soft, the cheese melted, and the bread crumbs browned.

Priceless Heirlooms

There are good tomatoes in the supermarket and good tomatoes in cans, but the best tomatoes are homegrown. Recently there has been a trend toward growing ancient varieties of tomato. These "heirlooms," as they are called, have more flavor—sweetness paired with acid—than ordinary tomatoes do. You can buy the seeds and grow them yourself, and some farmers markets have them too.

Apple-Cinnamon Crepes

The aroma of these delicious crepes will be sure to please children and adults alike. And yes, they taste as delightful as they smell. For a special treat, top them with wheat-free whipped cream or ice cream.

1. Preheat the oven to 350°F.

2. In a large skillet over medium heat, sauté the apples in butter for 20 minutes. Stir in cinnamon, cloves, and brown sugar.

3. Blend the cream cheese into the hot mixture.

4. Lay out crepes and place a spoonful of filling on each. Roll them and place in a baking dish prepared with nonstick spray.

5. Bake in oven until hot, about 8–10 minutes. Serve warm.

Serves 6

2 large tart apples, such as Granny Smith, peeled, cored, and chopped

1 tablespoon butter

1 teaspoon cinnamon

¼ teaspoon ground cloves

2 tablespoons brown sugar, or to taste

4 ounces cream cheese, at room temperature

12 Chestnut Flour Crepes (see recipe in this chapter), made with sugar

Dark Chocolate-Coconut Scones

Serves 8

1½ cups wheat-free, all-purpose flour

¼ cup coconut flour

½ teaspoon xanthan gum

¼ cup turbinado sugar

2 teaspoons wheat-free baking powder

⅛ teaspoon salt

¾ cup finely shredded coconut, unsweetened

½ cup coconut oil

2 large eggs

⅓ cup coconut milk

1 teaspoon wheat-free vanilla extract

¼ cup dark chocolate chunks or chips, wheat-free

Coconut or additional turbinado sugar for sprinkling (optional)

These wheat-free scones are perfect with a cup of coffee or tea. You can use carob chips to make them dairy-free as well.

1. Preheat the oven to 400°F. Line a baking sheet with parchment paper or use a silicone mat.

2. In a large bowl, mix together the flours, xanthan gum, sugar, baking powder, salt, and coconut. Work in the coconut oil until the mixture is crumbly.

3. In a separate bowl, whisk together the eggs, milk, and vanilla until frothy. Add to the dry ingredients, stirring until well blended. The dough will be sticky. Fold in the chocolate chunks.

4. Drop the dough onto the parchment paper or silicone mat and form into a circle in the center of baking sheet. Cut circle into 8 triangles.

5. Sprinkle the scones with coconut or turbinado sugar if desired. Bake for 15–20 minutes, or until golden brown. Remove from the oven and let cool for 5 minutes before serving.

Egg and Avocado Breakfast Burrito

Breakfast burritos are easy enough to prepare even on your busiest mornings. They are a great make-and-go breakfast food.

1. In a medium bowl, beat together the eggs, egg whites, cheese, and milk until frothy.

2. Heat the oil in a medium skillet over medium-high heat. Sauté the onion and green pepper until onion is translucent, about 2–3 minutes.

3. Pour the egg mixture into skillet and cook, stirring, until eggs are scrambled.

4. Season the mashed avocados with salt and pepper.

5. Place tortillas one at a time in a separate skillet and cook until warm, about 2–3 minutes.

6. Spread equal amounts of avocado on one side of tortillas and layer with equal amounts of goat cheese and scrambled eggs. Roll up into burritos and serve immediately with salsa on the side.

Serves 4

3 whole eggs
3 egg whites
¼ cup shredded Cheddar
    cheese
⅓ cup milk
1 tablespoon grapeseed oil
¼ yellow onion, finely chopped
½ green pepper, diced
2 avocados, peeled, pitted, and
    mashed
¼ teaspoon salt
½ teaspoon pepper
4 wheat-free corn or rice flour
    tortillas, warmed
⅔ cup crumbled goat cheese
¼ cup wheat-free salsa

Chocolate Chip-Zucchini Bread

Serves 8

2 eggs
½ cup turbinado sugar
½ cup grapeseed oil
½ cup unsweetened applesauce
1 tablespoon wheat-free vanilla extract
1 cup brown rice flour
½ cup almond flour
½ cup cornstarch
1 teaspoon xanthan gum
½ teaspoon baking soda
¼ teaspoon wheat-free baking powder
½ teaspoon salt
1 tablespoon cinnamon
¼ teaspoon ground cloves
¼ teaspoon nutmeg
1½ cups fresh zucchini, shredded
½ cup chocolate chips, wheat-free

You will never know that there are vegetables in this yummy bread—or that it's wheat-free. It's a perfect way to sneak vegetables into picky kids!

1. Preheat the oven to 350°F. Grease a 9" × 5" loaf pan with cooking spray.

2. In a large mixing bowl, beat together the eggs, sugar, oil, and applesauce. Add the vanilla and mix well.

3. In a separate bowl, combine the flours, cornstarch, xanthan gum, baking soda, baking powder, salt, cinnamon, cloves, and nutmeg.

4. Add the dry ingredients to wet ingredients and mix well.

5. Add zucchini and chocolate chips and stir to combine.

6. Pour into the greased loaf pan and bake for 60–70 minutes. Place a toothpick in center of bread and if it comes out clean, it's done.

Blueberry or Strawberry Pancakes

These are a healthy and delicious way to include a serving of fruit in your breakfast or brunch. You get some caramelization from the sugar and fruit—it's delicious. Top with more berries and whipped cream.

1. In a bowl, mix the fruit, sugar, and orange zest. Mash with a potato masher or fork.

2. Heat a griddle over medium heat. Add butter. Pour half-cupfuls of pancake batter on the hot griddle and spoon some berries on top.

3. When bubbles rise to the top of the cakes flip them over and brown on the other side.

Freezing Fruit in Its Prime

There's nothing like blueberry pie in January, and you don't have to use sugary canned blueberry pie filling. When fresh blueberries are available, just rinse a quart and dry on paper towels. Place the berries on a cookie sheet in the freezer for a half hour and then put them in a plastic bag for future use.

Makes 12 pancakes

½ pint blueberries or strawberries
1 teaspoon sugar
1 teaspoon grated orange zest
1½ tablespoons butter
1 batch Banana Pancakes batter
   (see recipe in this chapter)

No Grain Bread

Serves 12

2½ cups golden flaxseed meal
½ cup almond meal
1 tablespoon wheat-free baking
   powder
¼ teaspoon baking soda
1 teaspoon salt
1½ tablespoons sugar
1 teaspoon cinnamon
3 eggs, beaten
½ cup water
3 tablespoons extra-virgin
   olive oil

This bread is perfect for sandwiches, toast, or even grilled cheese. The flaxseed adds antioxidants and fiber, making this bread nutritious and delicious.

1. Preheat the oven to 350°F. Place parchment paper in a loaf pan.

2. In a large bowl, mix flaxseed meal, almond meal, baking powder, baking soda, salt, sugar, and cinnamon.

3. Add eggs, water, and oil to dry ingredients and combine well. Let batter set for 2–3 minutes to thicken up, then pour into the prepared pan.

4. Bake for about 20 minutes, until the top is brown, and the loaf springs back when you touch the top.

5. Cool and cut into slices. Store leftovers in the refrigerator to preserve freshness for up to 5 days.

Appetizers

Chapter 3

Tiny Chickpea Crepes

Serves 12

2 cups chickpea flour
2 cloves garlic, crushed
1 teaspoon wheat-free Tabasco
    sauce or other red hot sauce
1 teaspoon salt
1½ cups water
¼ cup olive oil, for frying

The chickpea (garbanzo bean) flour gives a slightly nutty flavor that goes well with many dips and fillings.

1. Mix flour, garlic, hot sauce, salt, and water in a blender, pulsing and scraping the mixture down the sides.

2. Heat the oil in a nonstick pan over medium-high heat. Add 1 tablespoon of the batter for 1½" crepes.

3. Cook until very crisp on the bottom, about 3–4 minutes. Do not turn. Remove from pan and place on paper towels or a platter. Now you can add fillings of your choice, cheese or vegetables, and close, or fold each crepe in half.

Rich in Soluble Fiber
Chickpeas (also called garbanzo beans) are rich in soluble fiber, which is the best type of fiber, actually helping to eliminate cholesterol from the body. Chickpeas are a good source of folate, vitamin E, potassium, iron, manganese, copper, zinc, and calcium. As a high-potassium, low-sodium food, they may help to reduce blood pressure.

Sicilian Eggplant Rolls

These make the perfect appetizer or entrée that will definitely impress your guests.

1. Cut the eggplant in very thin (⅛") slices with a mandoline or a vegetable peeler. Salt the slices and stack them on a plate; let sit under a weight for 30 minutes to let the brown juices out.

2. Pat the eggplant slices dry with paper towels.

3. Heat the oil in a large skillet or fry pan to 300°F. Dip the eggplant slices in rice flour and fry until almost crisp, about 2 minutes per side.

4. Drain the slices and then place a spoonful of the ricotta cheese and some chopped olives and garlic on the end of each slice. Roll and secure with a toothpick. Place in a greased baking pan.

5. Preheat the oven to 300°F. Sprinkle the rolls with Parmesan cheese and bake for 8 minutes. Serve warm.

Eggplant Makes a Great Wrap

Eggplant can be sliced thin lengthwise or crosswise and then fried, broiled, or baked. Salting and stacking eggplant slices under a weight will drain off the bitterness that some seem to harbor. Be sure to use a plate with steep sides or a soup bowl under the eggplant—it will release a lot of juice when salted.

Serves 6

1 medium eggplant (about 1 pound), peeled
Salt, as needed
1–2 cloves garlic, chopped
½ cup extra-virgin olive oil
½ cup rice flour
1 cup wheat-free ricotta cheese
¼ cup Sicilian olives, pitted and chopped
¼ cup freshly grated Parmesan cheese

Avocado-White Bean Hummus

Serves 10

1 (15-ounce) can cannellini beans, drained and rinsed
1 ripe avocado, pitted and diced
1 large clove garlic, coarsely chopped
¼ cup water, plus more as needed
Juice of 1 lemon
2 tablespoons extra-virgin olive oil
1 teaspoon kosher salt
2 tablespoons coarsely chopped fresh cilantro
Freshly ground black pepper, to taste

Simple yet impressive, this appetizer will wow your guests. It also makes a delicious and healthy alternative to mayonnaise on your favorite sandwich.

1. Place the cannellini beans, avocado, garlic, water, lemon juice, olive oil, salt, chopped cilantro, and pepper in a food processor fitted with a blade attachment or a high-speed blender.

2. Process until smooth, scraping down the sides of the bowl as needed. If the dip is too thick, pulse in more water, a tablespoon at a time, until the desired consistency is reached. Serve with Baked Corn Tortilla Chips (see recipe in this chapter).

Baked Corn Tortilla Chips

Who says tortilla chips have to be laden with fat and calories to taste good? These tasty chips are perfect with all kinds of dips and salsas.

Serves 6

24 large corn tortillas, wheat-free

1 teaspoon kosher salt

1. Preheat the oven to 350°F.

2. Cut tortillas into large triangular slices. Lay slices out in a single layer on a baking sheet and sprinkle with salt.

3. Bake 8–12 minutes, or until chips start to lightly brown. Repeat with remaining tortilla slices. Let cool for 10 minutes before eating.

Read the Label!

Some corn tortillas are made with wheat gluten! Thoroughly reading the labels will help keep you informed because sometimes they don't advertise that they contain wheat.

Classic Red Tomato Salsa

Serves 8

6 large, ripe, juicy red tomatoes
2 cloves garlic
2 jalapeño peppers, cored, seeded, and chopped
½ cup minced sweet white onion
Juice of 1 lime
1 teaspoon red wine vinegar, wheat-free
1 teaspoon salt
½ cup minced cilantro

Once you see how simple it is to make this homemade salsa, you will never want to buy the store-bought variety again! Serve with Baked Corn Tortilla Chips (see recipe in this chapter).

Place all the ingredients in a food processor and pulse until well blended. Do not purée. Refrigerate 1 hour or overnight before serving.

Salsa Style

Salsa is a Mexican invention, using the hot and sweet peppers, tomatoes, herbs, and spices available. Hot food has a purpose in a hot climate: it makes you sweat, and when you sweat, you cool off—a bit. Foods that are extremely hot do kill taste buds; so don't punish your mouth.

Light Gorgonzola and Ricotta Torte Appetizer

This appetizer is light and delicious. You will find that this works best in a springform pan. Serve warm or at room temperature.

1. Preheat the oven to 350°F.

2. Place the cheeses, oregano, lemon juice, zest, salt, and pepper in a food processor and process until very smooth.

3. Place the mixture in a bowl and fold in the beaten egg whites.

4. Spray the inside of a 10" springform pan with nonstick cooking spray. Add the cheese mixture, and bake for about 30 minutes or until slightly golden.

5. Sprinkle with the walnuts. Cool slightly and serve in wedges.

Serves 6

16 ounces fresh whole-milk ricotta cheese, wheat-free

4 ounces Gorgonzola cheese, crumbled

1 teaspoon fresh oregano, or ¼ teaspoon dried

1 teaspoon fresh lemon juice

1 teaspoon freshly grated lemon zest

1 teaspoon salt

½ teaspoon pepper

3 egg whites, beaten stiff

½ cup walnuts, chopped and toasted

Devilish Egg-Stuffed Celery

Serves 12

6 eggs, hard-boiled, cooled in
water, cracked, and peeled
2 tablespoons wheat-free
mayonnaise
6 drops wheat-free Tabasco
sauce
½ teaspoon freshly ground
white pepper
1 teaspoon celery salt
1 tablespoon wheat-free Dijon
mustard
2 tablespoons chopped onion
1 clove garlic, chopped
1 teaspoon salt
2 tablespoons half-and-half
4 stalks celery, washed and cut
into thirds

This is a different take on deviled eggs—you devil the whole egg. Try garnishing these eggs with 3 teaspoons salmon caviar, 3 teaspoons capers, 3 teaspoons green peppercorns, chopped fresh parsley, or hot or sweet Hungarian paprika.

1. Place all the ingredients except the celery in a food processor and blend until smooth.

2. Spread the resulting mixture into the celery and cover with foil or plastic wrap and chill for 1 hour.

3. Add garnishes of your choice just before serving.

An International Flavor
Chili sauce and mayonnaise will add a Russian flavor to the eggs. Salmon caviar as a garnish will add a Scandinavian touch. Change the amount of heat and the herbs and you will have a different taste sensation. Experiment to find the flavor combinations you like best.

Piquant Artichoke and Spinach Dip

This is the perfect dip for parties and entertaining. Serve with wheat-free corn or rice crackers or sliced vegetables.

1. Drain the thawed spinach, squeezing it with paper towels, until the extra liquid is gone.

2. Heat the olive oil in a large skillet over medium heat and add the spinach; cook until just soft, about 5 minutes.

3. Remove pan from heat and add the rest of the ingredients, stirring to mix. Serve warm or cold.

The Artichoke Quandary

Some people absolutely adore artichokes that come in cans or jars; others prefer fresh or frozen. Cooking artichokes requires a bit more work, but even a busy person can cook ahead. After cooking baby artichokes, you can use them in a number of ways, simply removing the outside leaves.

Yields 2 cups

1 (10-ounce) package frozen chopped spinach, thawed
2 tablespoons extra-virgin olive oil
1 (12-ounce) jar artichoke hearts, drained and chopped
4 ounces cream cheese
8 ounces wheat-free sour cream
2 cloves garlic, finely chopped
½ bunch scallions, chopped
2 tablespoons fresh lemon juice
¼ teaspoon freshly grated nutmeg
1 tablespoon freshly shredded or grated Parmesan cheese

Golden Parmesan Crisps

Makes 12 crisps

2 tablespoons unsalted butter
   (more if necessary)
12 heaping tablespoons
   coarsely grated fresh Parmesan cheese
1 teaspoon thyme
Freshly ground black or cayenne
   pepper, to taste

It's important to use a block of fresh Parmesan cheese for this recipe. The bottled stuff won't work as well because it's too fine and too dry. Using freshly grated ensures wheat-free as well. Use the coarse grating blade of a food processor or box grater.

1. Heat the butter in a large fry pan over medium heat until it bubbles.

2. Spoon the cheese by tablespoonfuls onto the butter, pressing down lightly with the back of the spoon to spread, making 12 tablespoon-sized crisps.

3. After about 2 minutes, turn and cook until both sides are lightly golden brown. Add more butter if necessary.

4. Sprinkle with thyme, black pepper or cayenne, or both. Serve at once.

Healthy Shrimp Scampi Appetizer

Shrimp scampi can be healthy and delicious. It's perfect on its own for an appetizer, or you can serve it over wheat-free noodles and steamed spinach for a complete entrée!

1. Heat oil in a 12" heavy skillet over medium-high heat until it simmers, then add the shrimp and sauté them, turning once, until just cooked through, about 2 minutes each side. Transfer shrimp with a slotted spoon to a large bowl.

2. Add the garlic, chicken broth, salt, and pepper to the skillet and bring to a boil. Continue boiling until the liquid is reduced to ½ cup, about 5–7 minutes.

3. Add the butter and stir until melted, then remove skillet from heat and stir in shrimp.

4. Add the mixture to a large bowl and toss with parsley and lemon zest. Squeeze lemon juice on top if desired.

Serves 6

3 tablespoons extra-virgin olive oil
1 pound cleaned, large shrimp, deveined and patted dry
4 cloves garlic, minced
1 cup reduced sodium, wheat-free chicken broth
¾ teaspoon salt
¾ teaspoon pepper
1 tablespoon unsalted butter
½ cup chopped parsley
½ teaspoon grated lemon zest
Juice of ½ lemon (optional)

Fresh Tomato and Basil Bruschetta over Porto-bellos

Serves 12

6 plum (Roma) tomatoes, seeded and chopped
2 tablespoons extra-virgin olive oil
½ red onion, finely chopped
4 cloves garlic, minced
2 tablespoons balsamic vinegar, wheat-free
3 tablespoons fresh basil, torn
1 tablespoon freshly grated Parmesan cheese
½ teaspoon salt
½ teaspoon pepper
6 large portobello mushroom caps, wiped clean, stems removed
Extra-virgin olive oil in Misto sprayer
8 ounces fresh mozzarella, thinly sliced

Don't use canned tomatoes or dried basil for this recipe. The fresh tomato and basil really make a difference. Serve as an appetizer, as a side dish, or in a salad.

1. Preheat the oven to 425°F.

2. In a large bowl, combine the tomatoes, olive oil, onion, garlic, vinegar, basil, and Parmesan cheese. Add salt and pepper and mix well.

3. Slice each mushroom cap in half, leaving two half circles, and place on a baking sheet sprayed with nonstick cooking spray. Lightly spray each portobello mushroom cap with Misto sprayer filled with olive oil. Bake for 5 minutes. Remove from oven.

4. Spoon bruschetta mixture on each mushroom half. Top with mozzarella and bake for 2–3 minutes, more until cheese is melted. Serve warm.

Tzatziki Dip

This Greek cucumber-yogurt dip is light and delightful with sliced vegetables.

In a medium bowl, mix all the ingredients together until thoroughly combined. Refrigerate for at least 1 hour to let the flavors settle in. Serve cold with sliced raw vegetables.

Tzatziki

Tzatziki—pronounced tsah-ZEE-kee—is a Mediterranean sauce made with yogurt and cucumbers. It is traditionally served as a meze (an appetizer). It is also used as a spread on gyros (Greek sandwiches) or souvlaki (Greek fast food consisting of meat and vegetables).

Serves 12

8 ounces plain Greek low-fat yogurt, wheat-free
2 tablespoons extra-virgin olive oil
1 tablespoon lemon juice
½ teaspoon salt
½ teaspoon ground black pepper
1 tablespoon fresh dill, chopped
2 cloves garlic, minced
2 tablespoons peeled, seeded, and minced English cucumber
1 tablespoon chopped fresh mint

Guacamole

Makes 1–1½ cups

3 medium Hass or 2 large, smooth-skinned avocados, peeled and seeded

Juice of 2 limes

½ cup finely minced sweet onion

½ cup grape or cherry tomatoes, halved

½ teaspoon wheat-free Tabasco sauce, or to taste

½ teaspoon salt, or to taste

2 tablespoons finely chopped fresh cilantro

⅛ teaspoon cayenne pepper, wheat-free (optional)

There are many recipes for guacamole. This a delicious recipe where the flavors unite wonderfully. Serve with Baked Corn Tortilla Chips (see recipe in this chapter).

1. In a large bowl, using a fork, mash the avocados.

2. Mix in the rest of the ingredients until well blended.

Choosing Avocados

Most store-bought avocados are hard as stones. That's fine; if you buy ripe ones, they generally have many blemishes. Just buy them a few days before you plan to serve them. Place them on a sunny windowsill or in a brown paper bag or wrap them in a newspaper. The paper seems to hasten ripening. The avocado should not have oily black spots in it when you cut it open but should be a uniform green. One or two black spots can be cut out, but don't use an avocado that is full of black spots or gray-brown areas.

Salads and Dressings

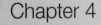

Chapter 4

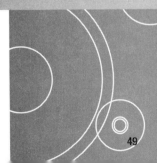

Apple, Walnut, Cranberry, and Spinach Salad

Serves 4

DRESSING

½ cup extra-virgin olive oil
½ cup balsamic vinegar, wheat-
   free
1 clove garlic, crushed
1 teaspoon ground mustard
1 teaspoon honey
1 teaspoon salt
½ teaspoon pepper

SALAD

1 (6-ounce) bag organic baby
   spinach
2 tablespoons chopped walnuts
2 tablespoons dried, unsweetened cranberries, wheat-free
1 Fuji apple, cored and chopped
½ medium orange bell pepper,
   seeded and chopped
2 plum tomatoes, chopped
½ cup kidney beans, thoroughly
   rinsed and drained
1 tablespoon chia seeds

The wonderful combination of fruit and nuts makes this salad perfect any time of year. The dressing can be used for any salad or as a marinade for chicken or vegetables.

1. Whisk all the dressing ingredients together in a small bowl. You can also pour into a small, airtight container and shake vigorously.

2. In a large bowl, mix the salad ingredients. Add the dressing and toss before serving.

Classic Caesar Salad

Caesar salad can be so versatile. Add chicken, shrimp, or even steak to dress it up as an entrée, or pair it with soup for an easy dinner.

1. Wash and spin-dry the lettuce; then chop, wrap in a towel, and place in the refrigerator to crisp.

2. In a large bowl, whisk together the egg, egg yolk, lemon juice, garlic, mustard, anchovy paste, and olive oil until very smooth. Add salt and pepper. Add the lettuce and toss.

3. Sprinkle with Parmesan cheese and croutons, and serve.

Not That Caesar

According to the JNA Institute of Culinary Arts in Philadelphia, Caesar salad was originally created in 1924 by Caesar Cardini, an Italian restaurateur in Tijuana, Mexico. The salad is named after its creator—a chef—not after Julius Caesar of the Roman Empire.

Serves 4

1 head romaine lettuce
1 whole egg and 1 egg yolk, beaten
Freshly squeezed juice of ½ lemon
2 cloves garlic, minced
1 teaspoon wheat-free English mustard
1" anchovy paste or 2 canned anchovies, packed in oil, mashed
¾ cup extra-virgin olive oil
1 teaspoon salt
½ teaspoon freshly ground black pepper
5 tablespoons freshly grated Parmesan cheese
24 Fresh Wheat-Free Croutons (see recipe in this chapter)

Fresh Wheat-Free Croutons

Serves 4

½ cup extra-virgin olive oil
2 cloves garlic, minced or put
  through a garlic press
4 slices wheat-free bread,
  thickly cut, crusts removed
1½ teaspoons salt
1 teaspoon black pepper
⅛ teaspoon red pepper flakes

These croutons can be made in advance and stored in the refrigerator, then crisped up at the last moment. They're the perfect addition to any salad.

1. Preheat the broiler to 350°F.

2. In a small bowl, mix the oil and garlic together. Brush both sides of the bread with the garlic oil. Sprinkle with salt, black pepper, and pepper flakes.

3. Cut each slice of bread into 6 cubes, to make 24 cubes. Spray a cookie sheet with nonstick spray. Place the cubes on the sheet and broil until well browned on both sides, 3–4 minutes each side.

4. Place the cookie sheet on the bottom rack of the oven. Turn off the oven and leave the croutons to dry for 20 minutes.

5. Store in an airtight container until ready to use.

For the Love of Garlic

Garlic will give you various degrees of potency depending on how you cut it. Finely minced garlic, or that which has been put through a press, will be the strongest. When garlic is sliced, it is less strong, and when you leave the cloves whole, they are even milder.

Wild Rice Salad

This salad is filling and flavorful any time of the year.

1. Bring water to a boil in a large saucepan or Dutch oven and add the rice. Return to a rolling boil and then reduce heat to simmer and cover tightly. After 30 minutes, add salt and pepper and remove from heat.

2. Add the onion, garlic, celery, water chestnuts, jicama, apple, and cranberries.

3. In a small bowl, whisk the olive oil and vinegar with the parsley. Pour over rice mixture and mix well.

4. Place salad in a large serving dish and serve warm or chilled. Top with raspberries at the last minute.

Cooking Wild Rice
Disregard the directions on the package of wild rice. They tell you to cook for 30–40 minutes, when it takes more like 90 minutes for it to bloom and soften. When cooking, just keep adding liquid if the rice dries out, and keep simmering until it "blooms" or the grains open up.

Serves 6

4 cups water
¾ cup wild rice
1 teaspoon salt
½ teaspoon black pepper
1 small red onion, chopped
1 clove garlic, finely chopped
3 stalks celery, finely chopped
1 cup water chestnuts, drained and chopped
1 cup jicama, peeled and chopped
1 small Gala apple, cored and chopped
1 tablespoon dried cranberries, unsweetened, wheat-free
⅔ cup extra-virgin olive oil
⅓ cup raspberry vinegar, wheat-free
½ cup chopped fresh Italian flat-leaf parsley
6 ounces fresh raspberries

Lemony Garlic Kale-Lentil Salad

Serves 6

1 tablespoon extra-virgin olive oil

3 cloves garlic, chopped

¼ cup chopped onion

2 cups kale, stems removed

½ cup sliced tomatoes

1–2 tablespoons fresh basil

½ teaspoon kosher salt

8 ounces lentils, soaked and cooked

2 tablespoons fresh lemon juice

2 tablespoons shaved Asiago cheese, or any other hard cheese

This light salad tastes wonderful the first day—and even better as leftovers. The lemon and kale create a delightful combination.

1. Heat oil in a large skillet over medium-high heat. Add the garlic and onion and sauté for 2 minutes.

2. Add the kale and tomatoes and sauté for 2–3 minutes more, until kale is softened but still crisp. Add basil and salt, and stir until blended.

3. In a large bowl, combine the kale mixture with the cooked lentils. Stir well.

4. Stir in lemon juice and cheese. Serve hot or cold.

A Valuable Source of Protein and Fiber

Lentils are an inexpensive way to get protein and fiber in your diet. They are also packed with crucial vitamins and minerals such as folate, vitamin B6, and magnesium, which are important for maintaining proper functioning of your body. Make sure you thoroughly rinse lentils before you cook them to ensure you have removed all dirt and debris.

Grilled Pear-Kale Salad with Feta Cheese

These grilled pears are wonderful along with the crisp texture of kale. Kale has become popular for its health benefits and delicious taste.

1. For the dressing, whisk together the lemon juice, 4 tablespoons oil, salt, and pepper in a small bowl. Set aside.

2. Prepare a grill to medium-hot heat (you should be able to hold your hand an inch over the cooking grate for 2–3 seconds). Make sure the cooking grate is well oiled.

3. Brush cut sides of pears with remaining grapeseed oil. Put pears, cut-side down, on the grill. Cover and cook until pear halves are grill-marked and heated through, about 10 minutes. Let them cool and slice into strips.

4. In a large bowl, add the kale, onion, cranberries, and walnuts. Stir to combine. Top with pears, feta cheese, and dressing.

Super Kale

Did you know that one serving of kale has 200 percent of your vitamin C daily requirement? Kale has even more vitamin C per serving than an orange! Kale is packed with fiber, vitamins, minerals, and antioxidants.

Serves 6

Juice of 1 small lemon
5 tablespoons grapeseed oil, divided
½ teaspoon coarse salt
½ teaspoon ground black pepper
4 pears, halved and cored, Bartlett or Bosc work best
4 cups finely chopped curly kale leaves
¼ red onion, finely chopped
1 tablespoon dried cranberries, unsweetened, wheat-free
¼ cup walnuts
¼ cup feta cheese

Three Bean Salad

Serves 8

1 (15-ounce) can black beans, thoroughly rinsed and drained
1 (15-ounce) can red kidney beans, thoroughly rinsed and drained
1 (15-ounce) can chickpeas (garbanzo beans), thoroughly rinsed and drained
1 green pepper, finely diced
2 medium red onions, finely diced
⅓ cup cider vinegar, wheat-free
¼ cup extra-virgin olive oil
1 clove garlic, finely diced
1 tablespoon honey
½ teaspoon ground mustard
½ teaspoon salt
½ teaspoon black pepper
Handful of fresh cilantro, chopped

This vegan salad is not too sweet and not too tangy like other bean salads. It tastes even better when marinated overnight.

1. In a large bowl, mix the black beans, red kidney beans, and chickpeas. Add the diced pepper and onions and mix well.

2. In a small bowl, combine the vinegar, oil, garlic, honey, mustard, salt, and black pepper. Once thoroughly mixed, pour over bean mixture.

3. Add cilantro and refrigerate for 3–4 hours before serving.

Tricolor Tomato-Bean Salad

Take advantage of local summer produce to create this perfect, light salad.

1. Place the tomatoes, cucumber, beans, and onion in medium-sized bowl.

2. In a small bowl, whisk together the oil, vinegar, garlic, and mustard until completely blended.

3. Pour oil and vinegar mixture over chopped vegetables. Stir to thoroughly combine. Refrigerate for at least 1 hour or overnight.

Visit Your Local Farmers' Markets

If available, your local farmers' market is the best place to buy the freshest fruit and veggies. Shopping at your local farmers' markets will not only support local farmers, but it will also stimulate your town's economy.

Serves 6

3 plum tomatoes, seeded and chopped
1 green tomato, seeded and chopped
1 yellow tomato, seeded and chopped
1 small cucumber, peeled and chopped into 1" wedges
1 (15-ounce) can small white beans, thoroughly rinsed and drained
½ red onion, finely chopped
3 tablespoons extra-virgin olive oil
2 tablespoons balsamic vinegar, wheat-free
2 cloves garlic, crushed
1 teaspoon wheat-free Dijon mustard

Grilled Corn Salad

Serves 8

4 ears un-shucked corn

2 avocados, peeled, pitted, and
cut into 1" squares

½ cup grape or cherry tomatoes,
halved

1 green pepper, diced

6 cups arugula, divided

Cilantro-Lime Vinaigrette (see
recipe in this chapter)

2 tablespoons fresh cilantro
leaves, torn

When you grill corn, it becomes juicy, sweet, and crispy. This salad is so simple and fla- vorful, you will want to make it again and again.

1. Pull back the husks of the corn and remove the silk. Pull husks back over corn. Lightly brush grates on grill with olive oil and heat grill to medium.

2. Place corn on the grill and cook for 15–20 minutes, turning occasionally. Remove from the grill and let corn cool.

3. When corn has cooled, shuck corn com- pletely. With a sharp knife, cut down sides of each corn cob to remove kernels, and place grilled corn kernels in a large bowl.

4. Add the avocados, tomatoes, pepper, and 3 cups of arugula to the bowl. Mix well.

5. Add Cilantro-Lime Vinaigrette and stir thor- oughly to combine. Refrigerate at least 1 hour to let the flavors soak in.

6. When ready to serve, place remaining 3 cups of arugula on a large platter and top with corn salad. Garnish with cilantro.

Tricolor Quinoa Salad with Vegetables, Cranberries, and Almonds

This salad is perfect for cookouts or potlucks when you want to have something a little different than your typical pasta or potato salad. This is definitely a crowd pleaser!

1. In a 2-quart saucepan, bring 2 cups water, the quinoa, and ½ teaspoon salt to a boil over high heat. Cover, reduce the heat to medium low, and simmer until the water is absorbed and the quinoa is translucent and tender, about 10–15 minutes. Immediately fluff the quinoa with a fork, and allow it to cool to room temperature.

2. In a sauté pan, place 1 tablespoon of oil with the carrots, artichokes, tomatoes, and spinach. Sauté until the vegetables soften, about 3–4 minutes. Add sliced almonds, and stir for 1 minute, until well mixed. Remove from heat.

3. Finely grate the zest from the lemon and then squeeze 1 tablespoon juice. In a small bowl, whisk the lemon zest and juice with the remaining tablespoon of olive oil, basil, cumin, paprika, and ¼ teaspoon salt.

4. In a large bowl, toss the lemon juice mixture with the quinoa, avocado, scallions, and cranberries.

5. Add the vegetable mixture, season to taste with salt and pepper, and serve.

Serves 4

1 cup uncooked tricolor quinoa, rinsed well and drained
¾ teaspoon kosher salt, divided, plus more for seasoning
2 tablespoons extra-virgin olive oil, divided
½ cup shredded carrots
1 (8.5-ounce) can artichokes, rinsed, drained well, and sliced
½ cup cherry tomatoes, sliced
1 cup baby spinach
2 tablespoons coarsely chopped toasted almonds
½ lemon
¼ teaspoon basil
¼ teaspoon ground cumin
¼ teaspoon sweet paprika, wheat-free
1 medium firm-ripe avocado, pitted, peeled, and cut into ½" chunks
1 medium scallion, white and light green parts only, thinly sliced
2 tablespoons cranberries
Freshly ground black pepper, to taste

Quinoa-Avocado Salad

Serves 8

1½ cups uncooked quinoa, rinsed and drained
3 cups water
2 (15-ounce) cans black beans, rinsed and drained
1 (14-ounce) box of frozen corn, defrosted
2 avocados, peeled and cut into ½" pieces
2 pints grape tomatoes, halved
Cilantro-Lime Vinaigrette (see recipe in this chapter)

This dish makes a hearty meal in itself or can be made as a side dish for chicken or fish. It tastes best when it is prepared the night before. Just make sure to save a little extra dressing to toss right before serving.

1. Cook the quinoa with the water according to package directions. Let cool to room temperature.

2. In a medium bowl, combine the beans, corn, avocados, and tomatoes. Toss with cooled quinoa.

3. Pour Cilantro-Lime Vinaigrette over the salad. Refrigerate for several hours or even overnight.

Cilantro-Lime Vinaigrette

This dressing is so wonderful you will want to make more of it and keep it in your refrigerator. It's perfect for all kinds of salads or even as a marinade.

Mix all ingredients together in a small bowl. Refrigerate until ready to serve. Store in an airtight container in the refrigerator for several days.

Cilantro, Love It or Hate It?

If you are among those who do not like cilantro, you are not alone. Feel free to substitute Italian parsley, mint, basil, or any other herb for cilantro in a recipe.

Makes 8–10 servings

1 clove garlic, minced
¼ cup grapeseed oil
¾ teaspoon minced fresh
  gingerroot
¼ cup fresh lime juice
Zest of 1 lime
2 teaspoons balsamic vinegar,
  wheat-free
¼ cup fresh packed cilantro
  leaves
Salt, to taste

Balsamic Quinoa Salad with Sweet Peppers and Feta Cheese

Serves 8

1½ cups uncooked quinoa, rinsed and drained

1 (15-ounce) can chickpeas, thoroughly rinsed and drained

1 yellow pepper, chopped

1 red pepper, chopped

½ medium red onion, minced

½ large cucumber, chopped

1 (6-ounce) container crumbled feta cheese

Chia-Balsamic Vinaigrette (see recipe in this chapter)

This really should be prepared the night before because the quinoa soaks up the dressing wonderfully.

1. Cook the quinoa according to instructions on the box. Place in large bowl when it is completely cooked.

2. Add the chickpeas, peppers, onion, cucumber, and feta to the quinoa as it is cooling off and mix well.

3. Add Chia-Balsamic Vinaigrette (see recipe in this chapter) and mix to combine. Chill for several hours, or overnight, before serving.

Grilled Portobello Mushrooms with Balsamic Glaze

This vegan salad is so filling and hearty any time of the year. If you haven't tried to grill portobellos, now is the time!

1. Place the arugula on a large platter.

2. Clean mushrooms and remove stems and any debris. Grill over a hot grill for 10 minutes, turning once. Place mushroom caps on top of the arugula.

3. In a small saucepan, heat the vinegar, sugar, and soy sauce to a boil. Reduce heat to low and simmer for about 15–20 minutes or until the mixture thickens. Remove from heat and let cool.

4. Once balsamic glaze has cooled a bit, pour evenly over portobellos and arugula. Serve immediately or at room temperature.

Serves 6

4 cups arugula, rinsed and dried
3 large portobello mushrooms
1 cup balsamic vinegar, wheat-free
1 tablespoon turbinado sugar
1 teaspoon wheat-free soy sauce

Greek Quinoa Salad

Serves 4–6

2 cups low-sodium chicken broth, wheat-free
1 cup uncooked quinoa, rinsed and drained
½ cup grape or cherry tomatoes, halved
½ cup chopped red or yellow sweet bell pepper
¼ cup chopped cucumber
2 teaspoons chopped pitted kalamata olives
1 tablespoon extra-virgin olive oil
½ teaspoon lemon zest
1 teaspoon fresh juice of lemon
1 teaspoon red wine vinegar, wheat-free
½ teaspoon basil, ground
½ teaspoon oregano
1 tablespoon garlic, minced
¼ cup feta cheese

This is a wonderful recreation of a classic Greek salad.

1. Heat the broth in a medium saucepan until it comes to a boil. Add quinoa and cover. Cook for 15–20 minutes, until all broth is absorbed. Remove from heat. Fluff with a fork.

2. Place the tomatoes, pepper, cucumber, and olives in large bowl. Set aside.

3. In a small bowl, combine the olive oil, lemon zest, lemon juice, vinegar, basil, oregano, and garlic. Mix thoroughly.

4. Add the quinoa to the vegetables and cover with the dressing. Top with feta cheese; stir to combine.

Chia-Balsamic Vinaigrette

You can make more of this dressing and keep it in your refrigerator. It goes well with veggies, meats, and any kind of salad.

1. In a clean, empty jar or Tupperware container with a lid, add the mustard, balsamic vinegar, oil, chia seed, salt, and pepper.

2. Add the chopped garlic along with the fresh basil leaves.

3. Cover the jar and shake well to blend. Store up to 5 days in airtight container.

Serves 6–8

1 tablespoon wheat-free Dijon mustard
5 tablespoons balsamic vinegar, wheat-free
1 tablespoon extra-virgin olive oil, or oil of your choice
1 tablespoon chia seed, ground
Salt and freshly ground black pepper, to taste
1 large garlic clove, finely chopped
1–2 tablespoons fresh basil leaves

Soups and Stews

Chapter 5

White Bean, Kale, and Turkey Sausage Stew

Serves 6

1 tablespoon grapeseed oil
½ cup chopped onion
1 (16-ounce) package wheat-
  free turkey sausage, cut into
  ½" slices
1 medium zucchini, quartered
  and cut into ½" slices
½ red bell pepper, chopped
3 cloves garlic, peeled and
  crushed
6 cups chopped, trimmed kale
  (about ½ pound)
½ cup fresh mushrooms,
  chopped
½ cup water
2 (16-ounce) cans cannellini
  beans or other white beans,
  rinsed and drained
3 Roma (plum) tomatoes
¼ teaspoon fennel
⅛ teaspoon dried chili flakes
½ teaspoon Italian seasoning
¼ teaspoon rosemary
¼ teaspoon salt
¼ teaspoon freshly ground
  black pepper

Who says comfort food has to be laden with
fat and calories for it to be comforting? This
dish is simple enough to prepare during the
week.

1. Heat oil in a large Dutch oven over medium-
high heat. Sauté onion and sausage 5–6 minutes or until sausage is browned.

2. Add the zucchini, pepper, and garlic, and
cook for 2 minutes.

3. Add kale and remaining ingredients; bring
to a boil. Cover, reduce heat, and simmer 10
minutes or until thoroughly heated. Serve
immediately.

Harvest Corn Chowder with Bacon

For this soup, fresh corn is best. Frozen or canned corn just won't taste the same. Fresh corn is sweet and crisp.

1. Fry bacon in a large skillet until crisp and drain on paper towels; when cool, crumble and set aside, reserving grease in pan.

2. Sauté the onions, potatoes, carrots, and pepper in the bacon grease for 10 minutes, stirring often.

3. Add the cornstarch/water mixture, and stirring constantly, ladle in the chicken broth. Bring to a boil. Cover, lower heat, and simmer for 30 minutes.

4. Stir in the rest of the ingredients. Taste, and season with salt and pepper. Do not boil after adding the cream. Serve hot, sprinkling the top with the crumbled bacon.

Serves 6

½ pound bacon, wheat-free
2 large sweet onions, finely chopped
2 large Idaho potatoes, peeled and chopped
½ large carrot, chopped
1 sweet red pepper, cored, seeded, and chopped
3 tablespoons cornstarch mixed with ¼ cup water until smooth
1 quart homemade or canned low-salt chicken broth, wheat-free
3 cups fresh corn removed from cob
1 tablespoon salsa, wheat-free
1 cup whole milk
1 cup heavy cream
¼ teaspoon ground nutmeg
1 bunch fresh parsley, washed, stems removed, chopped
Salt and pepper, to taste

Shrimp Bisque with Scallops

Serves 4–6

2 minced shallots

1 clove garlic, minced

2 tablespoons butter

2 tablespoons cornstarch

1 tablespoon tomato paste

4 cups shrimp shell broth (see sidebar in this chapter) or bottled clam broth, wheat-free

½ pound shrimp, cleaned and deveined

½ pound bay scallops

1 cup heavy cream

Salt and pepper, to taste

1 tablespoon dry sherry per bowl of soup

Chopped parsley, for garnish

This is an elegant first course or a delicious lunch. It's very easy to make in advance, adding the cream at the last minute when heating.

1. In a stock pot, sauté the shallots and garlic in the butter for 2–3 minutes.

2. Blend in cornstarch and tomato paste. Add broth and bring to a boil. Then lower heat and simmer for 10 minutes.

3. Spoon in the shrimp and scallops and cook for 2–3 minutes.

4. Let cool for 5 minutes. Using blender, blend in batches until puréed. Return to the pot and add cream. Taste for salt and pepper, adding as necessary.

5. Spoon in the sherry. Garnish with parsley.

Thick and Rich Cream of Broccoli Soup

This hearty soup is perfect on a cold, winter day. Feel free to add diced chicken or turkey to make it more of a meal.

1. Rinse, trim, and coarsely chop the broccoli; set aside in a colander to drain.

2. In a large soup pot, heat the oil or butter, and add onion, garlic, and celery. Sauté until softened, about 3–4 minutes.

3. Stir in the cornstarch/water mixture and other liquid ingredients.

4. Mix in the broccoli, nutmeg, juice and rind of lemon, salt, and pepper.

5. Simmer the soup, covered, until the broccoli is tender, about 15 minutes.

6. Remove the lemon rind. In blender, purée in batches, or use immersion blender directly in soup pot. Stir in the cream and ham. Reheat but do not boil. Serve hot.

Adding Depth of Flavor to Soup

Adding sausage, ham, or bacon to a soup enriches the flavor of soup. The salt and smoke in the curing process of pork plus the herbs and spices used in sausage also add to the flavor of a soup or stew. Smoked ham hocks are a classical tasty touch in Southern cooking. They are inexpensive and meaty, but the skin and bones must be removed before the soup is served.

Serves 4–6

1 pound broccoli
1 tablespoon extra-virgin olive oil or butter
1 large sweet onion, chopped
2 cloves garlic, chopped
1 stalk celery, chopped
2 tablespoons cornstarch dissolved in ⅓ cup cold water
3 cups low-salt chicken broth, wheat-free
½ cup dry white wine
¼ teaspoon freshly grated nutmeg
Juice and rind of 1 lemon
Salt and freshly ground pepper, to taste
1 cup heavy cream
¾ cup minced prosciutto or other smoked ham, wheat-free

New England Clam Chowder

Serves 4–6

2 dozen cherrystone clams (2" across)
3 ounces salt pork, finely chopped
1 large onion, chopped
1 medium carrot, peeled and chopped
2 stalks celery with tops, finely chopped
2 large Idaho potatoes, peeled and chopped
1 tablespoon cornstarch (more if you like it really thick)
2 bay leaves
½ teaspoon dill weed, dried
1 teaspoon dried thyme
1 teaspoon celery salt
1 tablespoon wheat-free Worcestershire sauce
3 cups clam broth, wheat-free
1 cup whole milk
1 cup cream
1 tablespoon cornstarch
Freshly ground black pepper, to taste
½ cup chopped fresh parsley, for garnish

This delightful chowder will warm you up on the chilliest winter days.

1. Scrub the clams and place them in a large pot. Add 2 cups water, cover, and boil until the clams open. Remove them to a large bowl and let cool; reserve the juice. When cool, remove the clams, discard the shells, and chop the clams in a food processor.

2. In a soup pot, fry the salt pork until crisp. Drain on paper towels. While reserving 1 table-spoon salt pork grease to cook vegetables.

3. Add the vegetables to the pot, and over medium heat, sauté until soft, about 10 minutes. Blend in the cornstarch and cook for 2 more minutes, stirring continuously.

4. Add the reserved clam juice, bay leaves, dill weed, thyme, and celery salt to the pot.

5. Stir in the Worcestershire sauce, clam broth, the chopped clams, and the salt pork. Bring to a slow boil before adding the milk, cream, and second tablespoon of cornstarch. Reduce the heat, cover, and simmer for ½ hour. After you add the milk and cream, do not boil. If you do, your soup is likely to curdle.

6. Taste and adjust seasonings, if necessary. Before serving, remove bay leaves. Add black pepper to taste and garnished with chopped fresh parsley, and serve hot.

Is That Clam Alive?

Never eat a dead clam. Always run them under cold water and scrub vigorously with a brush. To test for life, tap two clams together. You should hear a sharp click, not a hollow thud. If the clam sounds hollow, tap it again, and then, if still hollow-sounding, discard it.

Manhattan Red Clam Chowder

With tender chunks of clam, this savory dish will satisfy the seafood lover in your family.

1. Scrub the clams and place them in a large pot. Add 2 cups water, cover, and boil until the clams open. Remove them to a large bowl and let cool; reserve the juice. When cool, remove the clams, discard the shells, and chop the clams in a food processor.

2. In a soup pot, fry the salt pork until crisp. Drain on paper towels, while reserving 1 tablespoon salt pork grease to cook the vegetables.

3. Add the vegetables to the pot, and over medium heat, sauté them until soft, about 10 minutes. Blend in the cornstarch and cook for 2 more minutes, stirring continuously.

4. Add the reserved clam juice, bay leaves, dill weed, thyme, and celery salt to the pot.

5. Stir in the Worcestershire sauce, clam broth, the chopped clams, and the salt pork. Reduce the heat, cover, and simmer for ½ hour. Add the tomatoes. Cover and simmer for another ½ hour.

6. Before serving remove bay leaves. Add black pepper to taste and garnish with chopped fresh parsley, and serve hot.

Serves 6

2 dozen cherrystone clams (2" across)
3 ounces salt pork, finely chopped
1 large onion, chopped
1 medium carrot, peeled and chopped
2 stalks celery with tops, finely chopped
2 large Idaho potatoes, peeled and chopped
1 tablespoon cornstarch (more if you like it really thick)
2 bay leaves
½ teaspoon dill weed, dried
1 teaspoon dried thyme
1 teaspoon celery salt
1 tablespoon wheat-free Worcestershire sauce
3 cups clam broth, wheat-free
1 (28-ounce) can chopped tomatoes with their juice
Freshly ground black pepper, to taste
Parsley, chopped, for garnish

Tomato or Cream in Your Clam Chowder?

Manhattan clam chowder, made with tomatoes, is a latecomer to the chowder arena. During the eighteenth and nineteenth centuries, tomato-based chowder was banned in New England. In fact, tomatoes were suspect for many years—it was the invention and distribution of ketchup in the early twentieth century that brought the tomato into its own in America.

Summer Cucumber Soup

Serves 4

2 English cucumbers, peeled
and chopped
2 cups reduced fat buttermilk
1 cup Greek yogurt, wheat-free
2 teaspoons salt
Juice of 1 lemon
Rind of ½ lemon
⅔ tablespoon snipped fresh
dill weed
½ cup snipped fresh chives
(snipped to ¼" pieces)
Freshly ground pepper, to taste

This is very refreshing on a hot day. This soup is so simple to prepare, you can make an elegant and healthy summer soup in no time.

Mix all ingredients in a non-reactive ceramic or porcelain bowl. Chill overnight. Serve in chilled bowls.

Shrimp and Coconut Soup

This can be served chilled or hot. You can add 1 cup of cooked rice or quinoa to this, but it is not necessary.

1. Sauté the shallots in the oil until soft, about 10 minutes over medium heat. Stir in the cornstarch and cook until very thick.

2. Add the liquid ingredients and cook, covered, over very low heat for 30 minutes.

3. Stir in the rice or quinoa, and the shrimp; heat until the shrimp turns pink. Add basil, salt, and white pepper, to taste, and serve hot or cold.

Shrimp Shell Broth

Shrimp Shell Broth makes a flavorful addition to seafood soup. Next time you are preparing shrimp, reserve the shells. Add 1 cup of water, 1 cup of wine, and a bay leaf to the shells from a pound of shrimp. Bring to a boil, lower heat, and simmer, covered, for 20 minutes. Strain and use as broth in your soup.

Serves 4

2 shallots, minced

2 teaspoons peanut oil or other vegetable oil

2 tablespoons cornstarch

1½ cups homemade Shrimp Shell Broth (see sidebar), warmed

½ cup dry white wine

1 cup unsweetened coconut milk

1 cup cooked rice or quinoa (optional)

1 pound shrimp, shelled and deveined, chopped

1 teaspoon fresh basil, finely chopped

Salt and freshly ground white pepper, to taste

Thick and Hearty Lancashire Lamb Stew

Serves 6

¼ cup extra-virgin olive oil
2 pounds lamb stew meat
½ cup potato flour
Salt and pepper, to taste
2 slices bacon, chopped, wheat-
    free
4 cloves garlic
2 large onions, chopped
2 medium carrots, peeled and
    chopped
2 celery stalks, chopped
2 bay leaves
2 cups chicken broth, wheat-
    free
1 cup dry white wine
½ bunch parsley
2 tablespoons dried rosemary
Juice and zest of ½ lemon
2 teaspoons wheat-free
    Worcestershire sauce
1 (1-pound) bag great northern
    beans, soaked overnight and
    then simmered for 5 hours,
    or 3 (13-ounce) cans white
    beans, drained

This heart-warming stew freezes wonderfully so feel free to double the recipe and freeze half of it. You can also substitute canned cannellini beans for the bagged type.

1. Heat the olive oil in a big, heavy-bottomed stew pot.

2. Dredge the lamb stew meat with flour, salt, and pepper. Brown the meat, including the bacon for 5–8 minutes.

3. Add the garlic, onions, carrots, celery, and bay leaves and cook for 4–5 minutes.

4. When the vegetables are soft, add the broth, wine, and herbs. Stir in the lemon juice, zest, and the Worcestershire sauce. Cover and cook for 3 hours.

5. Pour off the broth and put in the freezer to bring the fat to the top. When the meat is cool enough to handle, remove from the bones.

6. Return the meat and broth to the pot. If too thin, mix 2 tablespoons of cornstarch with 3 tablespoons water and stir into broth. Bring to a boil.

7. Stir in the beans. Cover and cook at a simmer for 20 minutes.

Wild, Wild Rice and Mushroom Soup

The beauty of this rich, extremely comforting soup is that you can add more vegetables or cooked sausage, turkey, or chicken at the end.

1. In a soup pot, melt the butter, and add the garlic and onion. Sauté for 5 minutes.

2. Add the mushrooms. Add the flour or cornstarch, and stir until thickened, cooking for another 5 minutes.

3. Slowly add the broth, stirring constantly. Mix in the wild rice. Add the cream, rosemary, thyme, salt, and pepper, and allow to cook for another 2–3 minutes.

4. Add the sherry and serve in heated bowls, with a sage leaf floating in each one.

Serves 6

3 tablespoons butter
2 cloves garlic, minced
1 cup finely chopped sweet onion, such as Vidalia
10 each: shiitake, morel, porcini, and oyster mushrooms, brushed clean and chopped
2 tablespoons corn flour or cornstarch
5 cups low-salt, wheat-free, beef broth, heated
2 cups cooked wild rice
1 cup heavy cream
¼ teaspoon dried rosemary, crumbled
⅛ teaspoon dried thyme, crumbled
Salt and pepper, to taste
½ cup dry sherry
6 fresh sage leaves

Hot or Cold Asparagus Soup

Serves about 10–12

4 shallots, chopped

2 tablespoons extra-virgin olive oil

2 pounds fresh asparagus or 3 (10-ounce) packages frozen, cut into 1" pieces

2 quarts chicken broth, wheat-free

Salt and pepper, to taste

Juice of 1 lemon, and 1 teaspoon lemon zest

1 teaspoon wheat-free Tabasco sauce, or to taste

1 cup heavy cream

1 cup reduced fat milk

½ cup chopped fresh chives or mint leaves, for garnish

This delightful soup tastes just as good served hot or cold. This fresh, velvety soup has the most beautiful green color.

1. Using a large, heavy-bottomed soup pot, sauté the shallots in olive oil. When the shallots are softened after about 2–3 minutes, add the asparagus and toss for another 3–4 minutes.

2. Add the broth, salt, pepper, lemon juice and zest, and Tabasco sauce. Cover and cook until the asparagus is very tender, about 5 minutes.

3. Pour into a blender and process until very smooth, or use an immersion blender directly in soup pot. If you are going to serve it hot, reheat, add cream and milk, and serve. For a cold soup, chill, add cream and milk, and serve. Garnish with chopped fresh chives or mint leaves.

Spicy Mexican Black Bean Soup

This traditional soup is easy but takes quite a while to make. It freezes beautifully, so make a lot. If ham hocks are hard to find, or you would like a vegetarian option, add 1 teaspoon liquid smoke or smoked paprika (make sure it is wheat-free) at the end in place of the ham hocks.

1. In a large stock pot or Dutch oven, cover the ham hocks with cold water, bring to a boil, cover, and lower heat to simmer. Simmer for 4 hours. Cover the beans with cold water and soak overnight.

2. Remove the meat from the pot and reserve the cooking liquid. Remove the meat from the bones, discard the skin and bones, chop the meat, and set aside. Drain the beans. Add the beans to the reserved cooking liquid from the ham.

3. Stir the onion, garlic, beef broth, lime juice, vegetables, spices, and salt and pepper into the pot with the beans and cooking liquid. Add enough water to make 3½ quarts. Cover and simmer for 5 hours.

4. Stir in parsley or cilantro, taste for seasonings, and add additional salt and pepper if necessary.

5. Place mixture in the blender and purée the soup in batches, or use an immersion blender directly in soup pot. Return to the pot to heat. Return the meat to the pot.

6. Either add all of the rum at once and serve, or you can add it to individual bowls of soup. Top each bowl of soup with sour cream and a slice of lemon or lime.

Makes about 3 quarts

1 pound ham hocks, split
1 pound black beans, soaked in fresh water overnight
2 medium onions, chopped
4 cloves garlic, minced
2 cups beef broth, wheat-free
Juice of 1 fresh lime
1 large (½ pound) Idaho or Yukon Gold potato, peeled and chopped
2 medium carrots, peeled and cut up
2 jalapeño peppers, cored, seeded, and chopped
1 tablespoon ground cumin
½ teaspoon cayenne pepper, ground, wheat-free
1 tablespoon ground coriander
Salt and freshly ground black pepper, to taste
½ cup chopped fresh Italian flat-leaf parsley or cilantro
1 cup golden rum
Sour cream, wheat-free, and thinly sliced lemon or lime, for garnish

Steamy Oyster Stew

Serves 4

2 tablespoons unsalted butter

1 tablespoon shallots, minced

2 tablespoons wheat-free Worcestershire sauce

1 cup bottled or fresh clam broth, wheat-free

2 tablespoons cornstarch mixed with 3 tablespoons cold water

⅛ teaspoon cayenne pepper, wheat-free

1 quart shucked oysters, drained

2 cups milk

1 cup heavy cream or half-and-half to lighten it up

Sprinkle of celery salt and paprika

4 pats butter

Oyster crackers, wheat-free

This elegant and satisfying stew is lovely enough for entertaining.

1. Mix 2 tablespoons butter, shallots, Worcestershire, and clam broth together in a saucepan over medium heat for 3–4 minutes. Whisk in the cornstarch/water mixture. Add the cayenne pepper, oysters, milk, and heavy cream.

2. Heat carefully over a low flame until quite thick, stirring frequently for about 10 minutes.

3. Just before serving, sprinkle with celery salt and paprika, then float a pat of butter on top of each bowl. Serve with oyster crackers on the side.

Ostentatious Oysters

Oysters are loaded with zinc, iron, potassium, magnesium, and calcium as well as vitamins A and B12. They are also low in calories and high in protein. These nutritional advantages remain whether oysters are consumed raw or cooked.

Italian Sausage, Bean, and Vegetable Soup

There's nothing like a bowl of good soup, especially when you are in a hurry. This hearty soup can be made quickly and will not disappoint.

1. In a large skillet, sauté the sausage, onion, and garlic in the olive oil for 5–6 minutes.

2. When the onion and garlic are soft, add the rest of the ingredients, except the Parmesan cheese. Cover and simmer over very low heat for 30 minutes.

3. Garnish with Parmesan cheese and serve.

Serves 4–6

1 pound wheat-free Italian sausage, either sweet or hot, cut into 1" pieces
1 large red onion, chopped
4 cloves garlic, minced
¼ cup extra-virgin olive oil
1 (28-ounce) can crushed tomatoes with their juice
1 bunch of escarole, washed, base stems removed, chopped
2 (13-ounce) cans beef broth, wheat-free
2 (13-ounce) cans white beans
1 tablespoon fresh rosemary, crumbled
1 tablespoon dried oregano
⅓ cup freshly grated Parmesan cheese

Tasty Taco Soup

Serves 8

2 tablespoons extra-virgin olive oil

1½ pounds lean ground beef (you can also use ground turkey or chicken)

1 tablespoon extra-virgin olive oil

1 medium onion, chopped

3 cloves garlic, minced

1 red or yellow bell pepper, chopped

1 cup diced tomatoes

1½ cups frozen corn

1 tablespoon chili powder, wheat-free

¼ teaspoon red pepper flakes

¼ teaspoon oregano, dried

½ teaspoon paprika, wheat-free

1 tablespoon cumin

2–3 tablespoons fresh cilantro, chopped

Salt and pepper, to taste

1 (15-ounce) can red kidney beans, thoroughly rinsed and drained

1 can green chili peppers

3 cups chicken broth, wheat-free

1½–2 cups water (depending on how much liquid you want)

Juice of ½ lime

Cheddar cheese, wheat-free sour cream, extra cilantro, for garnish

This wonderful soup can be made into a chili if you reduce the amount of broth.

1. In a large stock pot or Dutch oven, heat 2 tablespoons oil and add the ground meat. Cook for 5–8 minutes, until completely browned and no longer pink. Remove from heat and place meat into a bowl.

2. In the same pot, heat the oil, onion, and garlic for 3–4 minutes, until they soften.

3. Add the bell peppers, tomatoes, corn, spices, and cilantro. Season with salt and pepper and mix well.

4. Add the kidney beans and chili peppers and mix again.

5. Add the meat back to the pot along with chicken broth, water, and lime juice. Mix well and bring to a boil.

6. Cover and reduce heat to low. Season with additional salt and pepper, if desired. Simmer for 30 minutes. Garnish with cheese, sour cream, and extra cilantro, if desired.

Do You Love Sour Cream?

If you are looking for a healthier alternative, why not substitute plain Greek yogurt for sour cream? Greek yogurt is also thick and creamy but has much less fat and fewer calories. Greek yogurt is also much higher in protein. Ensure the brand you choose is wheat-free.

Lentil-Spinach Soup

Nothing warms you up like a warm bowl of comforting soup loaded with healthy vegetables and beans. This freezes wonderfully so go ahead and double the recipe.

1. Heat the oil in a large pot over medium heat. Add the onions, garlic, carrots, celery, and zucchini and cook for 3–4 minutes, until vegetables soften.

2. Add oregano, basil, and cumin. Stir to combine and cook for 3–4 minutes.

3. Add tomatoes, lentils, vegetable broth, water, bay leaf, and Parmesan cheese rind, if using. Bring to a boil.

4. Reduce heat and let simmer 50–60 minutes, or until lentils are soft.

5. Right before ready to serve, add spinach and lemon juice. Stir well until spinach wilts.

6. Season with salt and pepper, if desired. Remove Parmesan cheese rind and bay leaf before serving.

For the Carnivores . . .

This is a delightful vegetarian soup. If you are a meat eater and are looking for a heartier soup, add some cooked wheat-free bacon, ham, sausage, chicken, or turkey at the end. You can add some small wheat-free noodles, potatoes, or corn as well for a more substantial meal.

Serves 6

1 tablespoon extra-virgin olive oil

2 medium onions, finely chopped

4 cloves garlic, minced

3 large carrots, chopped

3 stalks celery, diced

1 medium zucchini, diced

2 teaspoons oregano, dried

2 teaspoons basil, dried

1 teaspoon cumin

1 cup grape or cherry tomatoes, halved

1½ cups brown lentils, dried

4 cups vegetable broth (you can also use chicken broth), wheat-free

4 cups water

1 bay leaf

Rind of fresh Parmesan cheese (optional)

3 cups spinach

1 tablespoon lemon juice

Salt and pepper, to taste (optional)

Hearty Beef Stew

Serves 10

2 pounds beef stew meat, cubed

¼ cup all-purpose wheat-free flour

4 cloves garlic, minced

1 teaspoon onion powder

½ teaspoon black pepper, ground

2 tablespoons extra-virgin olive oil

3½ cups beef broth, wheat-free

2½ cups water

½ cup red wine

1 teaspoon wheat-free Worcestershire sauce

2 teaspoons marjoram, dried

1 teaspoon rosemary, dried

1 teaspoon parsley, dried

3 large red potatoes, peeled and cubed

4 large carrots, sliced and quartered

4 stalks celery, sliced

1 large onion, chopped

3 teaspoons cornstarch

2 teaspoons cold water

This heartwarming stew will leave you asking for seconds. If you like a thicker stew, add a bit more cornstarch.

1. Place the beef in a resealable plastic bag along with flour, garlic, onion powder, and black pepper. Make sure the bag is closed and shake until meat is evenly coated.

2. In a large pot or Dutch oven, place olive oil and flour-coated beef and cook over medium heat until browned, about 5–6 minutes.

3. Add broth, water, red wine, and Worcestershire sauce. Stir well and add marjoram, rosemary, and parsley. Bring to boil. Reduce heat to low, cover, and simmer for 1 hour.

4. Stir in potatoes, carrots, celery, and onion.

5. In a small bowl, mix together the cornstarch and water. Add mixture to pot and stir in well.

6. Cover again and simmer another 55–60 minutes, until potatoes soften. Serve immediately.

Cook It Slow

You can easily cook this stew in the slow cooker. Simply follow step 1, and then place beef and the remaining ingredients (except cornstarch and water) in slow cooker. Cook on low for 10–12 hours, or on high for 4–6 hours, adding the cornstarch and water mixture in the last hour.

Creamy Ham and Potato Soup

This is comfort food at its finest and is filling enough for an entrée. This is a great way to use leftover ham too. Go ahead and add whatever vegetables you'd like; cauliflower, asparagus, and corn would be delicious in this soup.

1. In a large stockpot, place the potatoes, onions, carrots, celery, ham, cayenne pepper, sage, parsley, garlic, broth, and water over high heat. Bring to a boil, then lower heat to medium, and cook for 15 minutes, until potatoes soften. Add salt and pepper to taste.

2. To make a roux, melt butter over medium-low heat in a medium saucepan. Slowly add flour, stirring continuously until thick, about 1 minute. Gradually add milk while continuing to stir. Continue stirring until thick and no lumps remain, about 4 minutes.

3. Stir the milk mixture into stock pot and mix well. Cook until thoroughly combined. Add shredded cheese, if desired, and garnish with chopped chives. Serve immediately.

What Is a Roux?

A roux is very simple to make and is crucial for thickening soups and sauces. A roux is prepared by using equal parts fat and flour and mixing them together until they are completely smooth.

Serves 8

- 3½ pounds Yukon Gold potatoes, peeled and diced
- 2 medium onions, chopped
- 2 medium carrots, sliced
- 2 celery stalks, diced
- 1 cup smoked ham, diced
- ⅛ teaspoon cayenne pepper, ground, wheat-free
- ½ teaspoon sage, dried
- 1 teaspoon parsley, dried
- 2 cloves garlic, minced
- 3 cups chicken broth, wheat-free
- 2 cups water
- Salt and pepper, to taste
- 4 tablespoons butter
- 5 tablespoons wheat-free, all-purpose flour
- 1½ cups milk
- ¼ cup shredded Cheddar cheese, for garnish (optional)
- Chopped fresh chives, for garnish

Slow Cooker Thai Curried Chicken Soup

Serves 6

2 pounds boneless, skinless
   chicken, cubed
½ teaspoon salt
½ teaspoon pepper
4 cloves garlic, minced
1 tablespoon fresh gingerroot,
   minced
1 tablespoon peanut oil
2 teaspoons red curry paste,
   wheat-free
1 teaspoon curry powder,
   wheat-free
1 teaspoon turmeric
1 teaspoon cumin
1 (14-ounce) can coconut milk
4 cups chicken broth, wheat-
   free
1 tablespoon fish sauce, wheat-
   free (optional)
Juice of 1 lime
1 jalapeño pepper, sliced
   (optional)
1 cup mushrooms, sliced
1 medium onion, chopped
1 red pepper, chopped
Sliced green onions and lime
   wedges, for garnish

This soup is packed with flavor. If you like it less spicy, cut down on the curry paste. Leftovers taste wonderful over a bed of rice or quinoa.

1. Salt and pepper the chicken breasts. Set aside.

2. Place the garlic, gingerroot, and peanut oil in a large skillet over medium-high heat and cook for 1–2 minutes, until tender.

3. Stir in the chicken and cook while stirring 5–8 minutes, until browned and no longer pink.

4. Place the cooked chicken in the slow cooker. Add the remaining ingredients to slow cooker except vegetables. Stir to combine. Cook on low for 6 hours.

5. Add vegetables including jalapeño and let cook another 30 minutes, until they soften. Garnish with sliced green onions and lime wedges.

Meat Dishes

Chapter 6

Tenderloin of Pork with Spinach and Water Chestnuts

Serves 4

2 pork tenderloins, about ¾ pound each
¼ cup potato flour
1 clove garlic, minced
¼ teaspoon nutmeg
¼ teaspoon ground cloves
Salt and pepper, to taste
¼ cup extra-virgin olive oil
2 tablespoons lemon juice
1 teaspoon wheat-free Worcestershire sauce
1 (8-ounce) bag fresh baby spinach or 1 (10-ounce) box frozen chopped spinach, thawed
½ cup sliced water chestnuts

For convenience, use fresh baby spinach, pre-washed and packed in a bag. This dish can be served with any variety of rice or roasted potatoes.

1. Trim the pork and cut into serving pieces. On a sheet of waxed paper, mix together the flour, garlic, and seasonings. Dredge the pork in the mixture.

2. In a large skillet, heat olive oil over medium heat and sauté the pork for about 6 minutes per side; it should be medium.

3. Add the lemon juice, Worcestershire sauce, spinach, and water chestnuts. Stir to wilt the spinach. Sprinkle with more olive oil, if the pan is dry.

Buying Pork

You can get "heirloom" or "heritage" pork on the web. Or you can get pork tenderloin in almost any supermarket. The tenderloin is about the best and juiciest cut available.

Garlic-Balsamic Crusted Pork Tenderloin

This is wonderful for entertaining. Mashed potatoes and roasted vegetables pair perfectly with this tenderloin.

1. In a small bowl, mix together the garlic, balsamic vinegar, mustard, salt, pepper, and olive oil. Rub the paste all over pork. Marinate for at least 2–3 hours or overnight if you'd like.

2. Preheat the oven to 400°F. Heat oil in large skillet over medium-high heat. Working in batches if necessary, add pork and brown tenderloin all over, about 4–5 minutes.

3. Transfer pan to preheated oven. Roast the pork, turning occasionally until the internal temperature reaches 160°F, about 20–30 minutes.

4. Transfer the pork to a cutting board and let rest 10 minutes before slicing. Top with fresh parsley if desired.

Serves 4

3 cloves garlic, minced
2 tablespoons balsamic vinegar, wheat-free
½ teaspoon ground mustard
1 teaspoon salt
¼ teaspoon pepper
1 tablespoon extra-virgin olive oil, for marinade
1–1¼ pound pork tenderloin
1 tablespoon extra-virgin olive oil, for sauté
2 tablespoons fresh parsley, for garnish

Baby Rack of Lamb with Herbed Crust

Serves 4–6

2 racks of lamb (1½–2 pounds each), most of the fat removed
2 teaspoons salt
Freshly ground black pepper, to taste
1 cup cornmeal
2 tablespoons dried rosemary, or 4 tablespoons finely chopped fresh
3 tablespoons minced fresh parsley
2 tablespoons minced chives
2 tablespoons minced garlic
½ green onion, finely minced
½ cup extra-virgin olive oil
6 sprigs fresh mint and lemon wedges, for garnish

The herbs and cornmeal give a delicious flavor in this dish and are a wonderful substitution for bread crumbs.

1. Preheat the broiler to 450°F.

2. Rub the lamb with salt and pepper. Place on a broiler pan, bone-side up. Broil for 5 minutes.

3. Turn and continue to broil for another 5 minutes.

4. While the lamb is broiling, mix the rest of the ingredients except mint and lemon together in a medium bowl. Press the herb mixture into the meat by making small incisions on top and pressing mixture into it and change the setting from broil to bake. Bake the lamb at 450°F for another 10–12 minutes.

5. Cut into chops and garnish with fresh mint and lemon wedges.

Mincing Chives

Of course, you can use a knife to mince chives; however, a pair of sharp kitchen scissors works faster and better than a knife. The scissors work well with any number of other ingredients too, such as scallions, bacon, and so on. As with any cutting tool, the sharper, the better—and safer. Dull tools are dangerous—they can slip off a tomato, for example—and can be inefficient.

Stuffed Filet Mignon with Red Wine Sauce

Stuffing a whole filet mignon with mush-rooms and garlic will turn it into a luscious feast. Using chestnut flour will add a nutty and delightful flavor.

1. In a large skillet over medium heat, melt the butter. Add the mushrooms, shallots, and gar-lic, and sauté until the vegetables are soft and the mushrooms are wilted, about 3–4 minutes.

2. Add the Worcestershire sauce. Add ¼ cup flour seasoned with salt and pepper and blend. Stir in ½ cup red wine and the sage, rosemary, and thyme. Reduce the mixture to about 1½ cups, about 5–7 minutes.

3. Preheat the oven to 350°F.

4. Make a tunnel down the middle of the filet mignon—use a fat knitting needle or the handle of a blunt knife. Stuff the mushroom mixture into the tube. If there are extra mush-rooms, save them for the sauce.

5. Coat the outside of the filet with ½ cup chestnut flour, salt, and pepper. Place the remaining beef broth in the bottom of a roast-ing pan with the filet. Sprinkle with olive oil and roast in oven for 20 minutes per pound.

Drippings Make the Perfect Sauce

Use the drippings for a sauce, served on the side. If the pan juices get too reduced, add some boiling water or more beef broth.

Serves 10–12

4 tablespoons unsalted butter
4 cups exotic mushrooms such as creminis, morels, shiitake, or oysters, brushed off, stems removed, finely chopped
6 shallots, peeled and minced
4 cloves garlic, peeled and minced
1 tablespoon wheat-free Worcestershire sauce
¼ cup chestnut flour, mixed with salt and pepper, to taste
½ cup dry red wine, divided
4 sage leaves, torn in small pieces
½ teaspoon dried rosemary
½ teaspoon dried thyme
1 (6-pound) filet mignon, fat trimmed
½ cup chestnut flour
1 tablespoon coarse salt
1 teaspoon black pepper
1 cup beef broth, wheat-free
2 tablespoons extra-virgin olive oil

Herb-Stuffed Veal Chops

Serves 4

½ cup minced shallots
½ medium onion, finely
   chopped
2 tablespoons chopped fresh
   rosemary
2 teaspoons dried basil, or 1
   tablespoon chopped fresh
   basil
½ teaspoon ground coriander
2 tablespoons unsalted butter
1 teaspoon salt
Pepper, to taste
4 veal rib chops, 1½"–2" thick,
   a pocket cut from the outside
   edge toward the bone in
   each
¼ cup extra-virgin olive oil
Salt and pepper, for outside of
   chops

This recipe calls for thick-cut chops. You can use double rib chops with a pocket for the aromatic herbs and vegetables. These can be grilled or sautéed.

1. In a skillet over medium heat, sauté the shallots, onion, and herbs in butter for 2–3 minutes. Add salt and pepper. Let sit for 5 minutes.

2. Stuff the chops with herbs. Rub chops with olive oil, salt, and pepper.

3. Using an outdoor grill or broiler, sear the chops over high heat, 1–2 minutes per side.

4. Cut heat to medium and cook the chops for 4–5 minutes per side for medium chops or rare chops, depending on the thickness.

Spicy Beef-Stuffed Mushrooms

The mushrooms should be 2½" across for this recipe. This is a great side dish or appetizer.

1. Sauté the meat, onion, garlic, gingerroot, and oregano in the oil, mixing constantly to break up lumps. When the meat turns pink (but not gray or brown), remove from the heat and add the Worcestershire sauce, taste, and add salt and pepper. When almost cool, blend in the egg.

2. Preheat the oven to 350°F. Divide the stuffing between the mushrooms in a baking pan. Pour enough water to come ¼" up the sides in the pan.

3. Bake the mushrooms for 25 minutes. You can sprinkle them with chopped fresh herbs of your choice when done.

Serves 4

½ pound chopped sirloin, lean
½ cup minced onion
2 cloves garlic, minced
1" piece gingerroot, peeled and minced
1 teaspoon ground oregano
2 tablespoons cooking oil
1 tablespoon wheat-free Worcestershire sauce
Salt and freshly ground black pepper, to taste
1 egg, slightly beaten
12–16 large mushroom caps, stems removed, brushed off

Greek Pork-Stuffed Eggplants

Serves 4 for lunch, or 8 as an appetizer

8 small eggplants, about 4"–5" in length
½ cup extra-virgin olive oil
½ cup minced onion
4 cloves garlic, minced
½ pound lean ground pork
Salt and pepper, to taste
½ cup fresh tomato, finely chopped
¼ teaspoon ground coriander
Juice of ½ lemon
Plain yogurt (wheat-free) and finely chopped tomato, for garnish

You can do most of this recipe in advance, refrigerate, and then put it in the oven for 10 minutes. This is wonderful over a bed of greens.

1. Preheat the oven to 400°F.

2. In a large skillet over medium-high heat, fry the whole eggplants in olive oil, for 5 minutes. Remove from pan and when cool enough to handle, make a slit from top to bottom but do not cut through.

3. In the same pan over medium heat, fry the onion, garlic, pork, salt, pepper, tomato, and herbs. Add the lemon juice.

4. Keep stirring to blend and break up the pork. Set aside to cool for 15 minutes.

5. Place the eggplants on a baking sheet that has been covered with aluminum foil. Spread the eggplants open, scrape the seeds out, and fill with pork stuffing.

6. Bake for 10 minutes. Serve with a dollop of yogurt on each eggplant and garnish yogurt with chopped tomato.

Stuffed Pork Chops

Ask the butcher for thick rib chops, and to slit a pocket in each. This will make stuffing the pork chops easier.

1. Sauté the apple, onion, and herbs in ½ cup olive oil over medium heat for 5 minutes.

2. Once the apples are softened, add the corn bread crumbs, salt, and pepper. Remove from heat. When cool enough to handle, stuff into the chops and secure with toothpicks.

3. Add ¼ cup olive oil to the pan and brown the chops over medium-high heat for 4–5 minutes each side. Add the rest of the ingredients, except for the cornstarch-and-water mixture, and cover. Simmer for 40 minutes over very low heat.

4. Remove the chops and place on a warm platter. Add the cornstarch-and-water mixture to the gravy in the pan if you want it to be thicker. Add salt and pepper to taste. Serve gravy either alongside the chops or poured over the chops.

Serves 4

1 tart apple, peeled, cored, and chopped
½ cup chopped onion
1 tablespoon dried rosemary, crumbled, or 2 tablespoons chopped fresh
¼ cup finely chopped Italian flat-leaf parsley
1 tablespoon dried basil
½ cup extra-virgin olive oil
½ cup wheat-free corn bread crumbs
Salt and pepper, to taste
4 thick-cut pork rib chops
¼ cup extra-virgin olive oil
4 cloves garlic, chopped
2 medium onions, chopped
½ cup chicken broth, wheat-free
½ cup dry white wine
Zest and juice of ½ lemon
2 ripe pears, peeled, cored, and quartered
2 teaspoons cornstarch mixed with 2 ounces cold water (to thicken the gravy)

Spicy Marinated Beef and Baby Spinach

Serves 4

2 cloves garlic, minced

2 tablespoons sugar

½ teaspoon salt, or to taste

1 teaspoon red pepper flakes, or
to taste

2 tablespoons canola oil

1½ pounds filet mignon,
trimmed and cut into ½"
slices

¼ cup dry white wine

¼ cup white wine vinegar,
wheat-free

2 teaspoons sugar

2 tablespoons fish sauce,
wheat-free

2 tablespoons canola or peanut
oil

½ green onion, finely diced

4 cups fresh baby spinach,
rinsed, spun dry, stems
removed

1 tablespoon butter

Wheat-free soy sauce, chopped
scallions, lemon or lime
slices, for garnish

After you have marinated the beef, the dish takes but a few minutes to cook. This dish will surely delight your guests.

1. In a large bowl or glass baking dish, mix together the garlic, 2 tablespoons sugar, salt, pepper flakes, and 2 tablespoons oil. Add the slices of filet mignon, turning to coat. Cover and refrigerate for 2 hours.

2. In a small bowl, mix together the wine, vinegar, 2 teaspoons sugar, and fish sauce; set aside.

3. When ready to cook, heat a nonstick pan over very high heat and add 2 tablespoons oil and green onion. Cook for 2 minutes.

4. Remove the meat from the marinade and add it to the pan. Quickly sauté the filets until browned on both sides, about 2 minutes per side. Arrange the meat over a bed of spinach.

5. Add the wine mixture and butter to the pan and deglaze, reducing quickly, about 1–2 minutes. Pour over the spinach and meat. Serve with soy sauce and chopped scallions on the side and slices of lemon or lime.

Fish Sauce

Fish sauce, available at Asian markets, is an important ingredient in Southeast Asian, Chinese, and Indonesian cuisines. It is extremely aromatic and it is important to remember that a little goes a long way in most recipes.

Sausage and Asparagus Risotto

This flavorful one-pot meal will leave you asking for a second helping. You can use turkey or chicken sausage as well.

1. In a large skillet over medium heat, cook the oil, onion, and garlic for 2–3 minutes, until onion becomes translucent.

2. Add the sausage links and cook while breaking them apart with a spoon. Once the sausages are browned, about 5–7 minutes, add mushrooms and stir for 1–2 minutes to combine.

3. Add rice and wine, and continue to stir and cook until liquid is completely absorbed, about 15–20 minutes.

4. Add chicken broth, 1 cup at time, while making sure all the liquid is absorbed before adding another cup.

5. After adding all the broth, add chopped asparagus and herbs, and continue to stir. When risotto is firm, yet creamy, it is finished. Top with grated Parmesan.

Serves 6

4 tablespoons extra-virgin olive oil
1 green onion, chopped
2 cloves garlic, minced
1 package of mild Italian sausage links, casings removed
2 cups shiitake mushrooms, wiped clean and stems removed
2 cups arborio rice
½ cup dry white wine or vermouth
5¼ cups low-sodium chicken broth, wheat-free
1 pound asparagus stalks, stems removed and cut into 2" pieces
1 teaspoon ground oregano
1 teaspoon ground basil
⅓ cup freshly grated Parmesan cheese

Ginger-Teriyaki Flank Steak

Serves 4

½ cup water
1 tablespoon sesame oil
½ teaspoon grated gingerroot
2 cloves garlic, minced
¼ cup wheat-free soy sauce
1 tablespoon honey
1 tablespoon cornstarch
1½ pounds beef flank steak

This Asian-inspired dish pairs perfectly with steamed vegetables and rice. This marinade can be used on a variety of meats such as chicken, pork, and other cuts of beef.

1. In a small bowl, mix water, sesame oil, gingerroot, garlic, soy sauce, honey, and cornstarch. Stir thoroughly to ensure the cornstarch has been mixed in well.

2. Place the steak in zip-top bag and pour the marinade on top. Make sure the bag is sealed and shake until well blended. Place in refrigerator and let sit for at least 4 hours or, even better, overnight.

3. When ready to cook the steaks, remove them from the bag and discard the leftover marinade.

4. Place steaks on preheated grill or on a grill pan and cook on each side for about 6–8 minutes, until you have reached your desired degree of doneness. The internal temperature should read at least 145°F.

Slice Against the Grain
Lines in the flank steak run from right to left down the length of the steak. By cutting across these lines, the knife will cut through the fibers, which makes it easier to chew. Slicing the steak on a 45-degree angle creates an elegant presentation.

Spicy Steak Fajitas

Skirt steak rubbed with spicy seasoning and chopped peppers and served with warmed corn tortillas makes for the perfect family meal.

1. In a small bowl, mix the cornstarch, chili powder, salt, paprika, red pepper flakes, Worcestershire sauce, lime juice, sugar, and cumin.

2. Rub the steaks with the garlic and the prepared seasoning mixture and then cut it into strips.

3. In a large skillet over medium heat, cook the onion, peppers, and cilantro for 3–4 minutes. Add steak strips and cook stirring frequently, until cooked through, about 7 minutes.

4. Remove from heat and spoon the meat into a corn tortilla. Top with cheese and roll them up.

Serves 8

1 tablespoon cornstarch
2 teaspoons chili powder, wheat-free
1 teaspoon salt
1 teaspoon paprika
½ teaspoon red pepper flakes
1 teaspoon wheat-free Worcestershire sauce
1 teaspoon fresh lime juice
1 teaspoon turbinado sugar
¼ teaspoon cumin
4 cloves garlic, minced
3 pounds skirt steak
½ green onion, chopped
1 green bell pepper, sliced
1 red or yellow bell pepper, sliced
½ bunch fresh cilantro
Corn tortillas, wheat-free
10 ounces shredded Monterey jack cheese

Healthy Goulash

Serves 8

2 pounds lean ground beef

2 large yellow onions, chopped

3 cloves garlic, chopped

3 cups water

2 (15-ounce) cans low-sodium tomato sauce

2 (14.5-ounce) cans diced tomatoes

1 tablespoon wheat-free soy sauce

1 tablespoon wheat-free Worcestershire sauce

2 tablespoons dried Italian herb seasoning (or 1 teaspoon each basil, oregano, rosemary, and thyme)

3 bay leaves

½ teaspoon dry mustard

1 teaspoon paprika

¼ teaspoon salt

2 cups uncooked brown rice noodles (preferably elbows)

¼ cup shredded white sharp Cheddar cheese

This one-dish meal is filled with flavor. This is not Hungarian Goulash, which is more of a beef stew with potatoes.

1. In a large Dutch oven, cook and stir the ground beef over medium-high heat, breaking the meat up as it cooks, until the meat is no longer pink and has started to brown, about 10 minutes.

2. Skim off excess fat, and stir in the onions and garlic. Cook and stir the meat mixture until the onions are translucent, about 10 more minutes.

3. Stir in water, tomato sauce, diced tomatoes, soy sauce, Worcestershire sauce, Italian seasoning, bay leaves, dry mustard, paprika, and salt. Bring the mixture to a boil over medium heat. Reduce the heat to low, cover, and simmer 20 minutes, stirring occasionally.

4. Stir in the macaroni, cover, and simmer over low heat until the noodles are tender, about 25 minutes, stirring occasionally.

5. Remove from heat, discard bay leaves, and top with shredded cheese. Mix well and serve.

Slow Cooker Pulled Pork

You will love how your house smells when this is slow cooking. Feel free to use chicken if you don't eat pork.

1. Place the onions, garlic, and broth in a slow cooker.

2. In a small bowl, combine the sugar, chili powder, salt, cumin, cinnamon, and oregano and mix well.

3. Pat the pork with a paper towel and rub the prepared mixture all over it. Place pork on top of broth in slow cooker.

4. In the same small bowl, mix the barbecue sauce and the soy sauce. Stir to combine. Pour on top of pork making sure the mixture is spread evenly on top. Cover and cook on low for 8 hours.

5. Remove pork from slow cooker and allow to cool slightly. If using bone-in pork, discard bone. Place pork in 9" × 13" casserole dish.

6. Shred the pork using a fork. Add additional barbecue sauce and slow cooker mixture if you'd like. Serve warm in wheat-free buns or tortillas.

Serves 6

2 medium yellow onions, chopped
5 cloves garlic, minced
1 cup beef broth, wheat-free
1 tablespoon brown sugar
1 tablespoon chili powder, wheat-free
2 teaspoons kosher salt
1 teaspoon cumin
½ teaspoon cinnamon
½ teaspoon dried oregano
1 (5-pound) pork shoulder, boneless or bone-in
1 cup wheat-free barbecue sauce
1 teaspoon wheat-free soy sauce

Fruit and Corn-Crusted Pork Tenderloin

Serves 4–6

6 dried apricots, wheat-free, chopped
½ cup dried cranberries, wheat-free
¼ cup white raisins (sultanas)
1 cup warm water
Juice of ½ lemon
2 pork tenderloins, about ¾ pound each
2 tablespoons wheat-free Worcestershire sauce
1 cup cornmeal
1 teaspoon salt
Freshly ground black pepper, to taste
½ cup extra-virgin olive oil

The colorful filling makes this a very pretty presentation. It also is delicious—and perfect for entertaining.

1. Put the dried fruit in a bowl with the warm water and lemon juice. Let stand until most of the water is absorbed, about 3–4 hours.

2. Preheat the oven to 350°F.

3. Make a tunnel through each tenderloin using a fat knitting needle or the handle of a blunt knife. Stuff the fruit into the tunnels.

4. Sprinkle both roasts with Worcestershire sauce.

5. In a small bowl, make a paste with the cornmeal, salt, pepper, and olive oil. Spread it on the pork.

6. Roast for 30 minutes. The crust should be golden brown and the pork pink.

Seafood

Chapter 7

Coconut-Lime Shrimp

Serves 4

1 egg
½ cup all-purpose, gluten-free flour
⅔ cup coconut milk
Juice from 2 limes
Zest from 1 lime
1½ teaspoons wheat-free baking powder
¼ cup plus 2 tablespoons coconut flour
1¼ cups finely shredded coconut
24 shrimp, deveined with tails on
½ cup grapeseed oil
Fresh lime wedges, for squeezing

This dish can be served as an appetizer or as a main dish on top of rice, quinoa, or a plate of wheat-free noodles.

1. In medium bowl, combine the egg, all-purpose flour, coconut milk, lime juice, lime zest, and baking powder.

2. Place ¼ cup plus 2 tablespoons coconut flour and shredded coconut in 2 separate bowls.

3. Hold shrimp by tail, and dredge in flour, shaking off excess flour. Dip in egg/milk mixture; allow excess to drip off. Roll shrimp in coconut, and place on a baking sheet lined with wax paper. Refrigerate for 30 minutes.

4. Heat oil in grill pan or skillet.

5. Sauté the shrimp in batches: cook, turning once, for 2–3 minutes, or until golden brown.

6. Using tongs, remove shrimp to paper towels to drain. Serve warm with fresh lime wedges.

Red Snapper in White Wine Sauce

This sauce can be used with any fish or meat, mashed potatoes, or rice. Feel free to adjust the amount of herbs or add some sliced mushrooms, olives, capers, or green peppercorns.

1. Season the fillets with salt and pepper on both sides.

2. In a skillet over medium heat, sauté the onion and garlic for 4 minutes in the butter and oil. Whisk in the cornstarch and cook for 3–4 minutes.

3. Whisk in the warm chicken broth, stirring until smooth. Then add the wine or vermouth. Swirl in the mustard and herbs. Simmer over low heat for 10 minutes, stirring occasionally.

4. While sauce is simmering, place 1 tablespoon olive oil in a skillet over medium heat. Add fish and cook approximately 3–4 minutes on each side. Pour the sauce over the top and serve hot.

Serves 2

2 (8-ounce) red snapper fillets
1 teaspoon salt
1 teaspoon ground black pepper
½ cup minced sweet onion
1 clove garlic, minced
2 tablespoons unsalted butter
1 tablespoon extra-virgin olive oil
3 tablespoons cornstarch
1 cup chicken broth, wheat-free, warmed
½ cup dry white wine or white vermouth
½ teaspoon prepared wheat-free Dijon mustard
¼ cup chopped parsley
1 teaspoon shredded fresh basil
½ teaspoon dried tarragon or rosemary
1 tablespoon extra-virgin olive oil

Crispy Beer-Battered Fried Shrimp

Serves 4

½ cup corn flour
¼ teaspoon salt
1 tablespoon butter, melted
1 whole egg
½ cup flat buckwheat beer
Old Bay Seasoning, to taste
1 teaspoon paprika, wheat-free
1¼ pounds shrimp, peeled and
   deveined
¼ cup golden rum
2 tablespoons wheat-free soy
   sauce
Light oil such as canola, for
   frying
1 egg white, beaten stiff

You can do everything in advance but fry the shrimp. Beer batter is delicious, but just be sure to use buckwheat beer. Don't be afraid of the name; buckwheat beer is actually wheat-free.

1. Make the batter in advance by mixing together the first seven ingredients (flour through paprika). Let stand for 1 hour.

2. Marinate the cleaned shrimp in rum and soy sauce for 20 minutes, covered, in the refrigerator.

3. Bring the oil for frying to 375°F. Add the egg white to the batter.

4. Dip the shrimp in the batter a few times to coat. In small batches, gently lower each shrimp into the oil. Fry for about 4 minutes, or until well browned. Drain on paper towels and serve.

Orange-Ginger Salmon

This is so simple and only has a few ingredients. This wonderful marinade can be used on various meats and fish.

1. Preheat the oven to 400°F.

2. Place orange juice, honey, and soy sauce in a small saucepan over medium low heat. Cook and stir 10–15 minutes, until reduced by about ½ and thickened. Remove from heat, and allow to cool.

3. Stir balsamic vinegar and gingerroot into orange juice mixture.

4. Line a baking pan with parchment paper. Place salmon fillets with the skin side down. Season with salt and pepper and pour half of the orange juice mixture on top of the salmon fillets.

5. Bake salmon for about 10–15 minutes until it easily flakes with a fork.

6. Cover the cooked salmon with the remaining orange juice mixture. Serve immediately.

All Salmon Is Not the Same

There are several varieties of salmon, with wild Alaskan salmon being the healthiest. Wild Alaskan salmon has a diet that is considered safe and healthy for the environment. Atlantic farm salmon may consume antibiotics and even food coloring. Always choose "wild salmon" over "farm salmon."

Serves 6

¾ cup orange juice
1 tablespoon honey
1 teaspoon wheat-free soy sauce
2 teaspoons balsamic vinegar, wheat-free
1 teaspoon finely chopped fresh gingerroot
2 pounds salmon fillet
Salt and ground black pepper, to taste

Seafood à la King

Serves 4

½ cup shallots, minced
1 tablespoon white onion, finely minced
1 clove garlic, minced
¼ cup unsalted butter
20 small white mushrooms, cut in half
20 pearl onions, fresh or frozen, cut in half
2 tablespoons cornstarch
2 ounces cold water
1 tablespoon tomato paste
2 tablespoons brandy
1½ cups cream
Salt and pepper, to taste
½ pound shrimp, cleaned and deveined
½ pound bay scallops
2 tablespoons red salmon caviar, for garnish

You can make the sauce the day before and add the seafood at the last minute. Serve with rice or stuff into crepes. This dish is fantastic for entertaining.

1. Sauté the shallots, minced onion, and garlic in the butter over moderate heat for 5 minutes. Add the mushrooms and pearl onions. Stir, cooking for 2–3 more minutes.

2. Mix the cornstarch with cold water and add to the pan, stirring to blend.

3. Blend in the tomato paste and brandy.

4. Warm the cream slightly, then stir it into the sauce in the pan. (You can prepare this dish in advance up to this point. Store in the refrigerator until ready to serve.)

5. Reheat the sauce but do not boil. Add salt and pepper to taste, then add the seafood. When the shrimp turns pink, the dish is done, about 3–4 minutes. Garnish with caviar and serve.

Long Live the King!

This dish was created at the Brighton Beach Hotel on Long Island, New York, by Chef George Greenwald for his boss, E. Clarke King, II. It became very popular when Campbell's came out with canned cream of mushroom soup, used as a base.

Sole Florentine

Sole is an adaptable fish; mild and sweet, it goes with many different flavors. Frozen spinach works fine for this. Just make sure you completely squeeze the water out.

1. In a skillet over medium heat, melt the butter and sauté the shallot and garlic until softened, about 5 minutes. Blend in the cornstarch, cooking until smooth.

2. Add the spinach, cream, and nutmeg. Cook and stir until thickened, about 3–4 minutes. Pour into a baking dish treated with nonstick spray and set aside.

3. Dip the pieces of sole in the beaten egg. Then, on a sheet of waxed paper, mix the flour, salt, and pepper. Dredge the sole in the flour mixture.

4. In a separate skillet, heat the olive oil over medium heat. Add the sole and sauté until lightly browned, about 2–3 minutes each side.

5. Arrange the sole over the spinach in the baking dish. Sprinkle with the cheese. Run under the broiler until very brown and hot, about 3 minutes.

Serves 4

3 tablespoons unsalted butter
1 shallot, minced
1 clove garlic, minced
3 tablespoons cornstarch
2 (10-ounce) packages frozen chopped spinach, thawed, moisture squeezed out
⅔ cup heavy cream
¼ teaspoon nutmeg
4 sole fillets, rinsed and dried on paper towels
1 egg, well beaten
½ cup rice or potato flour
Salt and pepper, to taste
⅔ cup extra-virgin olive oil
¼ cup freshly grated Parmesan cheese

Lobster with Sherry Sauce

Serves 4–6

4 chicken lobsters, 1–1¼
    pounds each
1 teaspoon Asian five-spice
    powder, wheat-free
1 clove garlic, minced
1 teaspoon parsley
¼ cup sesame seed oil
¼ cup sherry
Juice of ½ lemon
2 tablespoons minced ginger-
    root

This adaptation is a unique way to serve lobster. Garnish with fresh lemon wedges.

1. Boil the lobsters for 20 minutes, then split
them and crack the claws.

2. Preheat the broiler to 500°F.

3. In a saucepan, mix the rest of the ingredients together to make the sauce. Bring to a
boil and spoon over the lobsters.

4. Broil for 3 minutes. Serve.

Marseille Whipped Cod and Potatoes

You can use either salt cod or fresh cod in this dish. You can also substitute half-and-half for the milk or cream if you would like to lighten it up.

1. Soak the cod overnight in cold water to cover. Change water once or twice.

2. Boil the potatoes in their skins until a knife slides into the flesh easily. The timing varies by the size of the potato.

3. Using a long-handled fork, spear the boiled potatoes and peel them. Put the potatoes through a ricer and into a bowl. Whisk in the olive oil and the milk or cream, then add salt and pepper and basil and keep warm.

4. Steam the cod, salted or fresh, about 15 minutes, until very tender. Make sure there are no bones.

5. Place the cod in a food processor and process until smooth.

6. Fold the cod into the potatoes and mix in the chives and parsley. Blend with a fork until fluffy. Serve hot.

Serves 4

2 cups salt cod, or 1¼ pounds fresh cod
3 large or 4 medium potatoes, about 2 pounds
2 tablespoons extra-virgin olive oil
½ cup rich milk or light cream, use more or less depending on the consistency of the potatoes
Salt and pepper, to taste
1 teaspoon dried basil
½ cup each, chopped chives and parsley

Southern Fried Oysters

Serves 4

1 quart shucked oysters
½ cup corn flour
1 cup cornmeal
1 teaspoon wheat-free baking
  powder
¼ teaspoon nutmeg
½ teaspoon dried parsley
½ teaspoon salt, or to taste
Freshly ground black pepper,
  to taste
2 beaten eggs
Oil for deep-frying

These are so crunchy on the outside and succulent on the inside, you will probably have to make an extra batch. Best when served with a squeeze of fresh lemon juice.

1. Place the oysters in a colander to drain.

2. In a large bowl, thoroughly mix the flour, cornmeal, baking powder, nutmeg, parsley, salt, and pepper.

3. Dip the oysters in the beaten egg and then in the flour-and-cornmeal mixture.

4. Bring the oil in a pot to 375°F and fry for about 3–4 minutes or until browned.

5. Remove with a slotted spoon. Drain on paper towels.

Seafood Loves to Be Saucy

Even the tastiest of mollusks and crustaceans love to be dipped or bathed in sauces. And there are a variety of options and substitutions. Any citrus can be substituted for just about any other—for example, limes for lemons, grapefruit for orange, and you can blend them together for intriguing outcomes using your own original flair for flavors. Throw in some ginger, curry powder, or mustard, and you'll add another layer of flavor.

Golden Sautéed Diver Scallops

This recipe calls for pan-searing the scallops. It tastes wonderful. You'll find lots of excuses to serve these.

1. On a sheet of waxed paper, mix the flour, parsley, sugar, salt, and pepper. Roll the scallops in the flour mixture.

2. In a large skillet, heat the butter and oil over medium-high heat. Add the scallops and watch them. They will brown quickly. Cook for 2–3 minutes per side. Serve with any of your favorite sauces.

Serves 4

½ cup corn flour
½ teaspoon ground parsley
2 tablespoons white sugar
1 teaspoon salt
½ teaspoon white pepper
1½ pounds large diver scallops, each about 2" across
2 tablespoons unsalted butter
2 tablespoons extra-virgin olive oil

Baked Risotto with Seafood

Serves 6–8

3 tablespoons extra-virgin
olive oil
1 tablespoon butter
1 small onion, minced
1 clove garlic, minced
Salt and pepper, to taste
1 tablespoon fresh rosemary,
crushed, or 2 teaspoons
dried, broken up
1 teaspoon saffron threads
1 cup long grain rice
2½ cups chicken broth, wheat-
free
2 tablespoons Marsala or sherry
wine
1 pound raw shrimp, peeled,
deveined, and rinsed; or 1
pound bay scallops, rinsed;
or 1 pound crabmeat (not
imitation)

This is perfect for a dinner party where you want to impress your guests but don't want to spend all day making the risotto.

1. Preheat the oven to 350°F.

2. In a skillet over medium heat, heat the oil and butter. Add the onion and garlic, and sauté until softened for 2–3 minutes.

3. Add salt, pepper, rosemary, saffron, and rice, and mix to cover the rice with the oil. Add the broth, cover tightly, and place in the oven.

4. After the rice has cooked for 10 minutes, add the Marsala or sherry wine. Return to the oven and cook for another 10 minutes.

5. Add the shrimp or other seafood and continue to bake for 7 minutes more. Uncover and serve.

Crabmeat

There is a lot of crab and fake crabmeat around. The very best is Maryland blue crab, in lumps or flakes; it's also the most expensive, running up to $15 a pound. Fake crab, or surimi, is made from fish that has been cooked with the water and juices from crabmeat; it is cheap but many times is mixed with a wheat binder. Blue crabs are rounded and squat, unlike the gigantic, spider-like legs of Alaskan king crab, or the finger-like clusters of snow crab. There's nothing like a good fresh crab, whether from Alaska or Maryland.

Corn and Lobster Newburg

Have your fishmonger cook and remove the meat from three small (1¼ pounds each) lobsters, or buy frozen lobster meat. Serve with rice and salad.

1. In a skillet over medium heat, melt the butter and sauté the shallots and garlic for 5–6 minutes, until soft.

2. In a small bowl, beat the egg yolks.

3. Put the cream into a large pan over medium heat; scald the cream but do not boil. Remove from the heat.

4. Mix 2 tablespoons of hot cream into the beaten egg yolks and whisk vigorously.

5. Pour the egg mixture into the hot cream and return to the heat. Continue to whisk until thick. Add the corn and lobster. Heat, stirring, until very hot but not boiling. Add the sherry. Serve garnished with parsley.

Extra Egg Whites or Yolks

The recipe for Lobster Newburg calls for 4 egg yolks. This gives you the opportunity to make a marvelous dessert meringue with the whites. Or if you have a recipe that calls for whites and not yolks, you can make mayonnaise or custard with the yolks. There is a use for everything but the shells.

Serves 6

2 tablespoons unsalted butter
2 shallots, minced
1 clove garlic, minced
4 egg yolks
2 cups cream
1 cup fresh corn, cut off the cob, or frozen corn, blanched and drained
1½ pounds, or 4 cups, lobster meat
2 tablespoons dry sherry
2 tablespoons chopped parsley, for garnish

Cod Broiled on a Bed of Paper-Thin Potatoes

Serves 4

2 pounds of Idaho or Yukon Gold potatoes, peeled and sliced paper-thin

¼ cup extra-virgin olive oil

2 tablespoons butter, melted

Salt and pepper, to taste

4 cod fillets or steaks, about 5 ounces each

Salt, pepper, and butter for the fish

Chopped parsley and lemon wedges, for garnish

Cod is one of the world's most beloved and versatile fish. It can be baked, broiled, steamed, poached, salted, or cooked with milk in a stew. This dish is simple yet delicious.

1. Preheat the oven to 400°F.

2. In a baking pan that has been treated with nonstick spray, toss the thinly sliced potatoes with oil and melted butter, salt, and pepper.

3. Bake the potatoes for 40 minutes or until the top is brown and crisp and the inside soft.

4. When the potatoes are done, lay the fish on top, sprinkle with salt and pepper, dot with butter, and reheat the oven to broil.

5. Broil until the fish is done—8–10 minutes, depending on the thickness of the fish. If the potatoes start to burn, move the pan to a lower shelf in the oven.

6. Sprinkle with chopped parsley and serve with lemon wedges.

Parmesan Crusted Tilapia

These crispy tilapia fillets would be perfect served with rice and a green salad. Feel free to sprinkle extra freshly grated Parmesan cheese on top too.

1. Preheat the oven to 425°F.

2. Combine 1 tablespoon olive oil, bread crumbs, Parmesan cheese, seasonings, garlic, salt, and pepper in a medium-sized bowl. Stir to combine.

3. On a medium-sized plate, pour lemon juice.

4. Dip each fillet in lemon juice and then in the bread crumb mixture, to coat evenly on both sides. Place in baking dish that is well oiled. Sprinkle with remaining 1 tablespoon olive oil and additional Parmesan cheese, if you desire. Cover with aluminum foil so fish remains moist.

5. Bake for 20 minutes, or until the edges are browning. Take baking dish out of the oven and put the broiler on. Broil on medium for about 2 minutes so fillets get crispy.

Serves 2

2 tablespoons extra-virgin olive oil, divided
¼ cup wheat-free bread crumbs or cornmeal
¼ cup freshly grated Parmesan cheese
1 teaspoon dried basil
½ teaspoon dried oregano
½ teaspoon onion powder
½ teaspoon red pepper flakes
½ teaspoon dried rosemary
2 cloves garlic, minced
½ teaspoon salt
¼ teaspoon ground black pepper
1 tablespoon freshly squeezed lemon juice
3–4 tilapia fillets, depending on their size, washed and dried
Extra-virgin olive oil for baking dish; can use a Misto sprayer

Crispy Calamari

Serves 10

1–2 cups peanut oil for frying
(you may need more or less)
12 squid, cleaned and cut into
small rings
¼ cup cornmeal
¼ cornstarch
1 teaspoon sea salt
¼ teaspoon ground black
pepper
2 cloves garlic, minced
½ tablespoon parsley, dried
1 teaspoon oregano
¼ cup wheat-free bread crumbs
1 lemon, sliced into wedges, for
garnish

This lovely dish can be served as an appetizer served with Spicy Marinara Sauce (see Chapter 11), or it can make a wonderful addition to any salad. This recipe is very simple and delicious.

1. Preheat oil in a very large, deep-frying pan or wok. Oil must be very hot so let sit for a few minutes over medium heat.

2. While oil is heating, rinse squid with water and dry with paper towel. The calamari should be damp enough so the flour/bread crumbs will stick but not too damp or the mixture will clump.

3. In a medium-sized bowl, combine the cornmeal, cornstarch, salt, pepper, garlic, and seasonings. Dip the calamari rings into the batter, then coat with bread crumbs.

4. Deep-fry in small batches for 1–2 minutes, or until very light brown. Even if you think it may not be brown enough, stop cooking after 1–2 minutes or the calamari will be overcooked. Lay cooked calamari on paper towels to absorb any liquid. Serve with Spicy Marinara Sauce (see Chapter 11) or serve over a bed of greens in a salad.

Classic Creole Jambalaya

This traditional one-dish meal is easy and scrumptious.

1. Place the butter and sausage in a large pot or Dutch oven. Stir well and cook for 5–8 minutes, until sausage is fully cooked.

2. Stir in the paprika, cumin, cayenne pepper, oregano, and garlic. Cook for another minute until well combined.

3. Add the tomatoes, pepper, celery, onions, carrot, bay leaf, and salt.

4. Stir in the rice and broth, mix well, and bring to a boil. Cover and reduce heat to low. Let simmer about 50 minutes until rice is fully cooked and tender.

5. Add the shrimp and let cook about 5 minutes. Remove bay leaf before serving. Garnish with extra chopped onion and fresh parsley if desired.

Jambalaya a Different Way

There are so many variations of jambalaya these days. You could add chicken, ham, or even duck. Traditional Creole Jambalaya typically uses tomatoes and chicken broth, whereas Cajun Jambalaya typically uses no tomatoes, just broth.

Serves 4

2 tablespoons butter
8 ounces andouille sausage, wheat-free, cut into ¼ rounds
1 tablespoon paprika, wheat-free, ground
1 tablespoon cumin, ground
¼ teaspoon cayenne pepper, wheat-free
1 teaspoon oregano, dried
2 cloves garlic, minced
1 cup diced tomatoes
1 green pepper, seeded and diced
1 celery stalk, diced
3 green onions, sliced
1 large carrot, shredded
1 bay leaf
½ teaspoon salt
1 cup brown rice, uncooked
2 cups low-sodium chicken broth, wheat-free
1 pound large shrimp, peeled and deveined
Chopped fresh parsley (optional)

Fish Tacos with Tropical Fruit Salsa

Makes 12 tacos

½ teaspoon chili powder, wheat-free
1 teaspoon oregano, dried
2 cloves garlic, minced
1 teaspoon cumin
1 teaspoon cilantro, minced
½ teaspoon red pepper flakes
1 pound boneless cod fillets, fresh, or frozen and thawed
Juice of one lime
Salt and pepper, to taste
Tropical Fruit Salsa (see Chapter 15)
12 corn tortillas, wheat-free, warmed
Shredded lettuce, sliced avocado, wheat-free sour cream, extra cilantro, for garnish

These folded tacos can be stuffed with a number of different toppings. Although tacos originated from mainland Mexico, fish tacos are said to have derived from Baja California.

1. Preheat the oven to 375°F.

2. In a small bowl, mix chili powder, oregano, garlic, cumin, cilantro, and red pepper flakes.

3. Place cod fillets on a large sheet of aluminum foil and squeeze lime juice over top of them. With a spoon, sprinkle prepared seasonings on each side of the fillets. Season with salt and pepper. Fold the foil around the fish, and seal top to create a pouch. Place pouch on a baking tray.

4. Bake in the oven for 20 minutes or until fish easily flakes with a fork. Divide fish among the corn tortillas and top with Tropical Fruit Salsa.

Poultry

Chapter 8

Parmesan–Chia Seed Crusted Chicken

Serves 4

1 cup wheat-free, all-purpose
   flour
1 tablespoon fresh finely shredded Parmesan cheese
1 clove garlic, finely chopped
1 teaspoon dried basil
3 tablespoons ground chia
   seeds
1 egg
3 egg whites
4 boneless skinless organic
   chicken breasts

Chia seeds pack a nutritional punch in this chicken dish. You won't even miss the bread crumbs in this fantastic entrée.

1. Preheat the oven to 350°F.

2. Place the flour, cheese, garlic, basil, and chia seeds in a shallow bowl. Stir until well blended.

3. In another shallow bowl, whisk the eggs and egg whites until well blended.

4. Dip each chicken breast in egg mixture first, then dredge in flour/chia seed mixture until completely covered. Place in a 9" × 13" casserole dish.

5. Bake for 30–35 minutes, turning over halfway through the cooking time, until chicken is no longer pink.

Indian-Style Chicken with Lentils

In countries with huge populations, it's both wise and popular to stretch meat, fish, and seafood with all kinds of legumes.

1. Preheat broiler. Line a baking sheet with aluminum foil.

2. Place the lentils and water in a saucepan. Bring to a boil, reduce heat, and simmer.

3. Just before the lentils are cooked (when barely tender, after about 25 minutes), add ¼ teaspoon salt, pepper, garlic, onion, lemon juice, cumin, red pepper flakes, and parsley.

4. Toss the chicken with the yogurt, curry powder, remaining salt, and Tabasco sauce. Place chicken on foil-lined baking sheet and broil for 5 minutes per side.

5. Mix the chicken into the lentils and serve with rice.

Serves 4–6

1 cup lentils
3 cups water
½ teaspoon salt
1 teaspoon pepper
2 cloves garlic, peeled and
 minced
1 medium onion, peeled and
 finely minced
2 tablespoons lemon juice
1 teaspoon cumin
¼ teaspoon red pepper flakes
½ cup chopped fresh parsley
1 pound boneless, skinless
 chicken breasts, cut into
 bite-sized pieces
1 cup plain Greek low-fat yogurt,
 wheat-free
1 tablespoon curry powder,
 wheat-free
1 teaspoon wheat-free Tabasco
 sauce

Tasty Turkey Parmesan

Serves 4

1¼ pounds boneless, skinless turkey breast
1 cup wheat-free corn bread crumbs
1 clove garlic, chopped
½ teaspoon dried oregano
½ teaspoon dried basil
1 cup fresh Parmesan cheese, divided
1 egg
1 cup corn flour
1 cup extra-virgin olive oil
2 cups tomato sauce
½ pound whole-milk mozzarella, shredded or thinly sliced

Adding your favorite herbs and seasonings can modify this dish, which is a wonderful variation of the classic chicken Parmesan.

1. Preheat the oven to 350°F.

2. Flatten the turkey breast with a meat pounder. Cut into 4 serving pieces.

3. In a shallow bowl, mix the corn bread crumbs, garlic, oregano, and basil with ½ cup Parmesan cheese.

4. In another shallow bowl, beat the egg.

5. Pour the corn flour onto a plate. Dip the turkey in the flour, then in the egg, and finally in the crumb mixture.

6. Heat oil in a large skillet over medium-high heat. Fry turkey in oil until golden brown, about 4–5 minutes; drain on paper towels.

7. Spray a 9" × 13" baking dish with nonstick spray. Pour a little tomato sauce into the baking dish. Add the turkey pieces. Sprinkle with remaining ½ cup Parmesan cheese. Cover with tomato sauce. Spread the mozzarella over the top.

8. Bake in oven until hot and bubbling, about 20 minutes. Serve hot.

What's in the Stuffing?

The key to buying wheat-free food is reading every food label very carefully. Store-bought corn bread may have wheat flour mixed in with the corn flour and cornmeal. Corn muffins, also a favorite in making home-made bread crumbs or stuffing, can have a mixture of wheat flour and cornmeal. The safest way is to make the corn bread yourself.

Mexican Chicken and Rice

This dish is not too spicy, but it is well-seasoned. To save time, cook the rice while the chicken is simmering.

1. Mix the corn flour, salt, and pepper on a sheet of waxed paper. Dredge the chicken in it.

2. Heat the oil in a large frying pan or Dutch oven over medium-high heat. Brown the chicken, for 5–7 minutes. Remove the chicken from the pan and drain on paper towels.

3. Add the garlic, onion, tomatillos, hot pepper, sweet pepper, corn, and mushrooms. Sauté until soft, about 10 minutes.

4. Add the tomatoes, wine, lemon, and cinnamon. Mix well.

5. Return the chicken to the pan and add rice and broth. Bring to a boil. Then reduce heat to low, cover, and simmer for 45 minutes.

6. Just before serving, add the parsley or cilantro. Serve immediately.

Texas Influence

Mexican cooking is well seasoned, with layers of flavors coming from herbs, aromatic vegetables, and, yes, some spices. It's the Texas influence and the American passion for burning up the taste buds that has given Mexican cooking a reputation for being overly spiced.

Serves 4–6

½ cup corn flour
¼ teaspoon salt
½ teaspoon pepper
1 (3½-pound) chicken, cut in serving-sized pieces, rinsed and dried on paper towels
½ cup corn oil
4 cloves garlic, peeled and cut into thick slices
1 large red onion, chopped coarsely
4 tomatillos, peeled and chopped
1 hot pepper, such as serrano or poblano, cored, seeded, and chopped
1 sweet red pepper, cored, seeded, and chopped
½ cup frozen corn
10 mushrooms, chopped
1½ cups chopped fresh or canned tomatoes
1 cup dry red wine
1 lemon, thinly sliced, seeded
½ teaspoon cinnamon
1 cup short-grained rice, uncooked
3 cups cooked white rice
2 cups chicken broth, wheat-free
½ cup chopped flat-leaf parsley or cilantro

Sesame-Crusted Chicken Breasts

Serves 4

2 large boneless, skinless
  chicken breasts, halved
¼ cup pineapple juice
¼ cup orange juice
1 tablespoon lime juice
½ cup wheat-free soy sauce
1" piece gingerroot, peeled and
  minced
2 cloves garlic, or to taste,
  minced
1 teaspoon chili oil, or to taste
½ cup sesame seeds
1 tablespoon ground chia seed
1 egg, beaten
1 tablespoon vegetable oil

Serve this with rice and steamed vegetables. Leftovers can be chopped, mixed with a spicy wheat-free sauce, and used to fill Corn Crepes or Chestnut Flour Crepes (see Chapter 2) as a delicious snack.

1. Rinse the chicken breasts and pat dry with paper towels.

2. In a non-reactive bowl or glass pan large enough to hold the chicken, whisk together the juices, soy sauce, ginger, garlic, and chili oil.

3. Add the chicken to the sauce and turn to coat. Cover and refrigerate for 4 hours.

4. In a shallow bowl, mix the sesame seeds with ground chia seed.

5. Drain the chicken. Dip the chicken in the beaten egg and then in sesame seed mixture.

6. Heat oil in a large skillet over medium-high heat. Sauté breasts for 6 minutes per side. Serve hot.

Chili and Other Hot Sauces

Different kinds of chili are prepared in China, India, and other countries in Asia, Southeast Asia, and the Middle East. Chili oil is extremely hot. Chili paste comes in green and red and is popular in Thailand. The Chinese make a chili-and-garlic paste that is called Sichuan chili. Tabasco sauce, freshly chopped chilies (red and/or green), cayenne pepper, and red pepper flakes can be substituted. Check food labels to make sure the brand you choose is wheat-free.

Classic Southern Fried Chicken

Fried chicken is perfectly delicious for entertaining or for a quiet meal at home with the family.

1. Rinse the chicken pieces and dry on paper towels, then place in a resealable plastic bag with the buttermilk and marinate for 2–3 hours.

2. In a large paper bag, mix together the corn flour, garlic, salt, pepper, and baking powder. Add the chicken pieces to the corn flour mixture one at a time, then close the bag and shake until the chicken is well coated.

3. In a medium bowl, whisk the egg and beer together. Spread the cornmeal on a large piece of waxed paper. Dip the chicken in the beaten egg/beer mixture. Then roll in the cornmeal, pressing it down into the mixture.

4. Bring 1" of oil to 365°F in a fryer, or ½" of oil in a frying pan. Fry the chicken for 20–25 minutes, turning every 4–5 minutes. Watch the chicken carefully to make sure that it doesn't burn. Drain on paper towels.

Frying with Corn Flour

When you use corn flour or cornmeal for frying, you can mix it with either rice flour or potato flour for good results. For a light, tempura-like crust, try cornstarch mixed with water and egg as a coating. Wheat-free cooking does require a whole new chemistry.

Serves 4

1 (6-pound) chicken, cut into 8 pieces (drumsticks, thighs, breasts, and wings)
1 cup buttermilk
1½ cups corn flour
1 clove garlic, chopped
1 teaspoon salt
1 teaspoon black pepper
1 teaspoon wheat-free baking powder
1 egg, beaten
½ cup wheat-free, buckwheat beer
1½ cups cornmeal
½ cup vegetable oil

Chicken Cacciatore

Serves 4–6

1 cup potato or corn flour
¼ teaspoon salt
½ teaspoon pepper
¼ cup fresh basil, torn, or 2
  tablespoons dried basil
1 teaspoon oregano, crumbled
1 (3½-pound) chicken, cut into
  8 pieces
¼ cup extra-virgin olive oil
1 teaspoon butter
1 medium onion, peeled and
  diced
2–3 cloves garlic, peeled and
  minced
2 tablespoons fresh rosemary
2 cups mushrooms, brushed off
  and chopped
1 (16-ounce) jar wheat-free
  marinara sauce or 16 ounces
  canned tomatoes
4 ounces dry red table wine
½ cup fresh Parmesan cheese
1 bunch fresh parsley, chopped

This classic, tasty dish can be served over rice or spaghetti squash.

1. In a large bowl combine the flour, salt, pepper, basil, and oregano. Dredge the chicken in the mixture.

2. In a large frying pan over medium-high heat, heat the oil and butter together until butter melts.

3. Brown chicken in butter and oil, for 5 minutes per side.

4. Add the onion, garlic, rosemary, and mushrooms. Sauté for 5 minutes.

5. Add the marinara sauce (or tomatoes) and red wine. Cover and simmer over very low heat for 1 hour.

6. Remove cover, place chicken on a platter, and continue to simmer sauce until reduced by half, about 15 minutes.

7. Spoon sauce over the chicken and sprinkle with cheese and fresh parsley.

Easy Turkey Meat Loaf

This is classic comfort food. Serve with roasted or mashed potatoes and roasted vegetables. You can also use ground chicken or beef for this recipe. For an extra touch, drape 2 slices of bacon over the top of the meat loaf before cooking.

1. Preheat the oven to 350°F.

2. Place all the ingredients into the large bowl of a food processor, and process together.

3. Treat a 9" × 5" bread pan with nonstick spray. Pour in the meat loaf mixture.

4. Place a roasting pan in the middle of the oven. Add 1" of hot water to the roasting pan. Place the bread pan containing the meat loaf in the water. Bake 80 minutes.

A Hot Water Bath

Baking your meat loaf in a hot water bath enables it to stay juicy. Processing the ingredients makes a much smoother meat loaf than the coarse stuff that you have to chew for a long time. The water bath is called a *bain-marie*, and it keeps baked foods soft, creamy, and moist.

Serves 6–8

1½ pounds lean ground turkey
½ cup chili sauce, wheat-free
½ cup milk
3 eggs
1 cup wheat-free corn bread crumbs
Salt and pepper, to taste
2 cloves garlic, minced
1 small onion, minced
1 teaspoon dried rosemary, crumbled
2 teaspoons Lea & Perrins steak sauce
½ teaspoon nutmeg

Elegant Duck and Fruit-Filled Corn Crepes

Serves 4

½ cup chicken broth, wheat-free

1 tablespoon cornstarch

⅔ pound boneless, skinless duck breasts

½ cup corn flour

4 tablespoons unsalted butter

½ teaspoon salt

2 teaspoons freshly ground black pepper

½ cup dried cranberries, wheat-free, soaked in ⅔ cup apple juice or wine

¼ cup dried cherries, wheat-free, soaked in ½ cup orange juice

¼ cup chopped celery tops

24 pearl onions

1 tablespoon rosemary leaves, dried and crumbled

½ teaspoon dried thyme

½ cup apple brandy (such as Calvados)

8 large Corn Crepes (see Chapter 2)

This would be a delicious dinner or lunch served over baby spinach or fresh salad greens. The sweetness of the duck works with the fruit—a marriage made in heaven.

1. In a small bowl, mix the chicken broth and the cornstarch and set aside.

2. Dredge the duck breasts in the corn flour.

3. Heat 2 tablespoons butter over medium heat. Sauté the duck breasts for 3–4 minutes, turning once.

4. Add the salt and pepper and the chicken broth/cornstarch mixture to the pan, stirring to make a sauce.

5. Add the soaked fruit, celery tops, onions, rosemary, thyme, and apple brandy. Cover and cook for 20 minutes over low heat.

6. Preheat the oven to 350°F.

7. Cool and remove the duck from the pan. Cut it into small pieces and shred. Return the duck to the sauce. Divide the duck and sauce mixture between the 8 crepes. Roll the crepes, place them, seam-side down, in a greased baking dish.

8. In a small saucepan, melt the remaining butter and drizzle over the crepes. Heat in the oven for 10–15 minutes.

Thai Chicken with Peanut Dipping Sauce

The chicken or other meat for satay should be grilled over hot coals. You can use tender beef instead of chicken. The marinade is perfect with any meat.

1. Make the dipping sauce: In a food processor, combine the coconut milk, peanuts, lemon or lime juice, brown sugar, soy sauce, ginger, and chili oil. Process until very smooth.

2. Heat the peanut oil in a large saucepan. Add the onion and garlic, and cook over medium heat until just soft, about 3 minutes. Pour the peanut mixture into the pan and mix well. Heat on low for 2–3 minutes but do not boil. Set aside.

3. Set 12 (10") skewers to soak in water to cover for at least 40 minutes.

4. Rinse the chicken, pat it dry, and cut it into bite-sized pieces.

5. Mix the rest of the chicken ingredients together and add to the chicken in an airtight container. Cover and marinate for 2 hours.

6. String the chicken on the skewers and grill over glowing coals for 4–5 minutes per side. Serve with wheat-free dipping sauce.

Wooden Skewers Must Be Soaked!

Wooden skewers must be soaked, or they will burn when on the grill or under the broiler. Place them in a pan of water for an hour. You can also get very fancy skewers with decorative handles or metal at the ends. Simple metal skewers are also available. When using metal skewers, be sure to oil them or use nonstick spray to keep the food from sticking.

Serves 4

Dipping Sauce

½ cup unsweetened coconut milk

1 cup dry-roasted peanuts

1 tablespoon lemon or lime juice

1 tablespoon dark brown sugar

1 tablespoon wheat-free dark soy sauce

1 teaspoon fresh ginger, minced

½ teaspoon chili oil

2 tablespoons peanut oil

2 tablespoons finely chopped sweet onion

2 cloves garlic, minced

Chicken

1½ pounds boneless, skinless chicken breast

½ cup wheat-free soy sauce

1 tablespoon coconut milk

2 teaspoons wheat-free Thai red chili paste, or to taste

2 tablespoons minced fresh gingerroot

1 tablespoon sesame oil

2 tablespoons dry sherry

Roasted Cornish Game Hens with Ginger-Orange Glaze

Serves 4

2 Cornish game hens, split open
2 tablespoons extra-virgin
  olive oil
½ teaspoon salt
¾ teaspoon pepper
1 tablespoon orange marmalade
2 tablespoons peanut oil
1 tablespoon wheat-free soy
  sauce
2 tablespoons orange juice
½ medium white onion, finely
  chopped
1 tablespoon minced fresh
  gingerroot

This is simple and tastes fantastic. It tastes just as delightful as leftovers the next day.

1. Preheat the oven to 375°F.

2. Rinse the hens, pat dry with paper towels, brush with olive oil, and sprinkle with salt and pepper.

3. In a small saucepan over low heat, stir the rest of the ingredients together to make glaze; set aside.

4. Roast the hens in a baking dish or pan, cut-side up, for 15 minutes. Turn hens and brush with glaze. Continue to roast for another 20 minutes, brushing hens with glaze every 5 minutes. Serve with roasted vegetables, rice, or mashed potatoes.

Fresh Gingerroot

You can use fresh gingerroot in all kinds of dishes, from dinners to desserts. Dried ground ginger, ginger snaps, and candied ginger are often used in cooking. Unpeeled fresh ginger freezes beautifully and can be added to sauces, salad dressings, and desserts such as puddings. When you want to use it, cut off an inch or two and peel it, then grate it, mince it, or chop it finely.

Ginger, Soy, and Kale Chicken

This recipe has a wonderful combination of ginger and soy. Marinate it the night before to let the chicken thoroughly absorb the flavors.

1. In a small bowl, whisk together the soy sauce, sesame oil, honey, gingerroot, and garlic.

2. Place chicken in a zip-top plastic bag and pour half of the soy mixture into bag. Make sure the bag is closed and shake it up so all the chicken is covered. Let marinate for at least a half hour or overnight.

3. Remove chicken from the marinade. Heat olive oil in a skillet over medium-high heat. Sauté the chicken for 5–8 minutes, until fully cooked and no longer pink.

4. Add the kale and cook until it is still bright green but only a little soft, about 2 minutes. Add remaining soy mixture and mix well.

Are You Familiar with Kale?

Kale is a powerhouse of nutrition as well as being a member of the cabbage family. Kale is packed with fiber, calcium, vitamin B_6, vitamin A, vitamin K, and vitamin C. Kale can be eaten raw or cooked and can replace your other leafy greens in all varieties of recipes.

Serves 2

4 tablespoons low-sodium wheat-free soy sauce
1 tablespoon toasted sesame oil
1 tablespoon honey
½ teaspoon freshly grated gingerroot
2 cloves garlic, crushed
2 boneless, skinless organic chicken breasts, cut into 1" cubes
1 tablespoon extra-virgin olive oil
2 cups kale

Hot and Spicy Turkey Meatballs

Makes 10–12 meatballs

1 pound lean ground turkey
2 eggs
2 cloves garlic, minced
1 teaspoon dried oregano
1 teaspoon dried basil
½ teaspoon cinnamon
½ teaspoon fennel seeds
½ cup fresh finely grated
    Parmesan cheese
2 cups crushed low-salt potato
    chips, wheat-free, divided
½ teaspoon salt
½ teaspoon pepper
4 tablespoons canola oil

Meatball recipes usually include bread crumbs as a filler and sometimes for an out-side coating. This recipe uses ground potato chips. The eggs will hold the meatballs together, and who doesn't love potato chips?

1. In a large bowl, mix the turkey, eggs, garlic, oregano, basil, cinnamon, fennel seeds, cheese, potato chip crumbs, salt, and pepper.

2. Place a large sheet of waxed paper on the counter. Sprinkle remaining cup of chip crumbs on it.

3. Form 1" meatballs from the turkey mixture. Roll meatballs in crumbs to coat.

4. Heat oil in a large skillet over medium-high heat. Fry meatballs until well browned, about 5 minutes. Drain on paper towels and then either refrigerate, freeze, or serve with the marinara sauce of your choice.

Kick Up Those Meatballs
You can add flavor to your meatballs by grinding up some wheat-free sweet or hot Italian sausage and mixing it with the beef. A truly great Italian sausage has aromatics like garlic and herbs, and spices such as anise seeds.

Spicy Olive Chicken

The key to this flavorful dish is simmering while covered for a while. Don't forget to pour the extra sauce on top of the chicken and over your side dish as well.

1. Sprinkle the chicken pieces with ¼ teaspoon salt and ¼ teaspoon pepper. Heat butter in a skillet over medium-high heat. Brown chicken pieces for about 5 minutes per side. Remove from pan and set aside.

2. In the same pan, sauté the garlic and onion for 5–10 minutes, until onions are soft. Add the broth, wine, and olives. Using a fork, whisk in the mustard.

3. Return chicken to the pan. Cover and simmer until the chicken is done, about 45 minutes. Add hot sauce and remaining salt and pepper.

4. Pour sauce and olives over mashed potatoes, rice, or rice noodles. Garnish with chopped parsley and capers.

Capers

Capers are flavorful berries. Picked green, they can be packed in salt or brine. Try to find the smallest—they seem to have more flavor than the big ones do. Capers are great on their own or incorporated into sauces. They are also good in salads and as a garnish on many dishes that would otherwise be dull.

Serves 4

1 (3-pound) chicken, cut into 8 pieces
½ teaspoon salt, divided
½ teaspoon pepper, divided
4 tablespoons unsalted butter
2 cloves garlic, chopped
⅔ cup chopped sweet onion
½ cup chicken broth, wheat-free
½ cup dry white wine
24 green olives, pitted
1 teaspoon prepared wheat-free Dijon mustard
¼ teaspoon wheat-free hot sauce
Fresh parsley, chopped
1 tablespoon capers

Chicken Piccata

Serves 8

1 cup low-sodium chicken broth, wheat-free

½ cup dry white wine or vermouth

2 tablespoons lemon juice

4 skinless, boneless chicken breasts sliced in half

½ teaspoon salt

½ teaspoon ground black pepper

1 tablespoon butter

½ medium onion, chopped

4 cloves garlic, minced

1 (13.75-ounce) can artichoke hearts, rinsed and drained

4 tablespoons capers

2 tablespoons freshly minced flat-leaf parsley

½ lemon, thinly sliced

This zesty, traditional Italian dish is packed with flavor and has become extremely popular in restaurants. Serve it with rice or wheat-free pasta.

1. In a small bowl, whisk together the broth, wine, and lemon juice. Set it aside.

2. Place a halved chicken breast between two pieces of plastic wrap. Using the flat side of a mallet, pound each breast until about ¼" thick.

3. Remove the top of the plastic wrap and sprinkle one side of the chicken with half of the salt and pepper.

4. Heat butter in a large skillet over medium heat. Place chicken in the skillet with the salt and pepper side down. Add remaining salt and pepper to the other side.

5. Cook chicken about 4 minutes per side, until no longer pink in the middle. Remove chicken from the skillet and place on a plate. Keep warm.

6. Add broth mixture, onion, and garlic to the same skillet; cover and reduce heat to low. Let simmer for 5–10 minutes until liquid reduces to about half.

7. Add browned chicken, artichoke hearts, and capers. Let simmer on low heat, uncovered, for a few minutes so sauce thickens. Top with parsley and lemon slices.

Orange Chicken Lettuce Wraps

Crisp lettuce makes a perfect, crunchy wrap for this mildly orange teriyaki chicken.

1. Heat 1 tablespoon oil in large skillet over medium heat. Add the onion and gingerroot, and sauté a few minutes, until onion becomes translucent, about 2–3 minutes.

2. Add the chicken and stir-fry until no longer pink, about 8–10 minutes. Remove from skillet.

3. In a large bowl, whisk the remaining oil, soy sauce, red pepper flakes, garlic, teriyaki sauce, vinegar, orange juice, and honey.

4. Add the cooked chicken, carrots, and water chestnuts and mix until thoroughly combined.

5. Serve chicken mixture in lettuce leaves to make individual wraps.

Serves 6

2 tablespoons canola oil, divided
½ green onion, chopped
1 tablespoon gingerroot, minced
1 pound boneless, skinless chicken breasts, rinsed and cut into 1" cubes
1 tablespoon wheat-free soy sauce
½ teaspoon red pepper flakes
1 clove garlic, chopped
2 tablespoons wheat-free teriyaki sauce
2 tablespoons rice vinegar, wheat-free
½ cup orange juice
1 tablespoon honey
1 cup shredded carrots
½ cup chopped water chestnuts
12 large lettuce leaves, iceberg or Bibb

Fiesta Lime-Lentil Salad

Warm Chickpea Salad with Spinach

Indian Vegetable Cakes

Spinach, Tomatoes, and Gnocchi in Classic Pesto Sauce

Classic Pesto Sauce

Pesto, Arugula, and Yellow Tomato Pizza with Cauliflower Pizza Crust

Cauliflower Pizza Crust

Corn and Spinach Pockets Stuffed with Cheese and Artichokes

Tofu and Vegetables with Macadamia Nuts and Asian Citrus Sauce

Stuffed Portobello Mushrooms

Classic Polenta with Herbs and Parmesan

Broccoli and Cheese-Stuffed Baked Potatoes

Potato Frittata with Cheese and Herbs

Stuffed Eggplant with Ricotta and Spices

Classic Italian Risotto

Vegetable Lasagna Primavera with Pasta Substitute

Spinach, Kale, and Mushroom Pizza

Vegetarian

Chapter 9

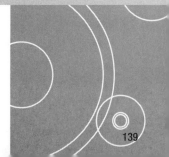
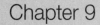

Fiesta Lime-Lentil Salad

Serves 8

1 (16-ounce) bag of dried lentils
4 cups water
½ teaspoon sea salt
2 tablespoons freshly chopped
cilantro
1 tablespoon grapeseed oil
½ cup broccoli, chopped
¼ cup carrots, sliced
½ cup green cabbage, chopped
¼ cup radish, chopped
½ green pepper, chopped
1 celery stalk, chopped
2 cloves garlic, minced
¼ teaspoon ground chili pepper,
wheat-free
½ teaspoon dried oregano
1 teaspoon dried basil
1 teaspoon dried cumin
½ teaspoon dried paprika,
wheat-free
½ teaspoon ground cayenne
pepper, wheat-free
Juice of 1 lime

This is the perfect meatless dish that even carnivores will love.

1. Rinse the lentils under running water and pick through them to remove any bits of soil or rocks.

2. Add the lentils and water to a saucepan (with a lid) and bring to a boil. Turn heat down to low and cover to let the lentils simmer, but leave the lid ajar a bit so that they don't boil over. Check on them occasionally to make sure the water has not boiled down below the level of the lentils; add more water as needed. When the lentils are tender and can easily be mashed with a fork, they are done. It usually takes about 30–45 minutes for them to cook.

3. Add salt and cilantro in about the last 15 minutes of cooking time—when the lentils are starting to get soft. (Cooking often neutralizes the taste of the salt, so if you add it at the start you end up having to add more salt to get the same flavor.)

4. When they are finished cooking, take the saucepan off the heat and cover tightly with the lid. Leave to sit for 5–10 minutes. The lentils will absorb more of the water making them juicier and more tender.

5. In a skillet over medium heat, add the oil and chopped veggies and sauté for 5 minutes.

6. Add lentils and seasonings and stir. Let sit on medium-low heat for 5–8 minutes until the veggies soften.

7. Remove from heat, add fresh lime juice, and stir until well blended.

Warm Chickpea Salad with Spinach

Chickpeas (or garbanzo beans) are loaded with protein and fiber. If you use canned beans, make sure you rinse them thoroughly before using. Serve this with a side green salad for a balanced meal.

1. Heat the olive oil in a skillet over medium-low heat. Cook the garlic and onion in the oil until translucent, about 5 minutes.

2. Stir in the spinach, chickpeas, cumin, salt, and curry. Continue to stir for a few minutes. Add lemon juice and broth, and stir. Allow to cook until thoroughly heated.

The Benefits of Beans

Beans are low in fat and help regulate blood sugar levels. They are also high in dietary fiber, which studies have shown can help lower cholesterol, reduce blood pressure, and support proper digestive health.

Serves 4

1 tablespoon extra-virgin olive oil
4 cloves garlic, minced
½ onion, diced
2 cups fresh baby spinach
1 (12-ounce) can chickpeas, rinsed and drained thoroughly
½ teaspoon cumin
½ teaspoon salt
⅛ teaspoon curry powder, wheat-free
Juice from ½ freshly squeezed lemon
¼ cup vegetable broth (or chicken broth), wheat-free

Indian Vegetable Cakes

Serves 4–6

1 tablespoon extra-virgin olive oil

1 (10-ounce) package frozen chopped spinach, thawed and squeezed of excess moisture

5-ounces frozen baby peas, thawed

½ bunch scallions, chopped

1 teaspoon curry powder, wheat-free

½ teaspoon turmeric

½ teaspoon ground black pepper

Salt and wheat-free hot pepper sauce, to taste

¼ cup cornmeal

5 extra-large eggs, well beaten

½ cup freshly grated Parmesan cheese

This is a great way to get kids to eat their veggies! A nonstick pan helps prevent sticking. Wheat-free sour cream makes a very good garnish.

1. Heat olive oil in a nonstick pan over medium heat.

2. In a large bowl, mix together all the ingredients except the Parmesan cheese. Form into patties.

3. Drop patties, 3 or 4 at a time, into the pan and fry until delicately browned, 3–4 minutes per side. Turn and sprinkle with cheese before serving.

Terrific Turmeric

Do you know about the health benefits of turmeric? Curcumin, a main ingredient in turmeric, has been shown to reduce inflammation. Some studies indicate that it may help ease the pain and symptoms of arthritis and rheumatoid arthritis. Other research shows that turmeric may protect against diseases, such as certain cancers, Alzheimer's disease, high cholesterol, and heart disease, to name a few. Try adding turmeric to your favorite dishes for some added health benefits.

Spinach, Tomatoes, and Gnocchi in Classic Pesto Sauce

This meal is so simple to prepare that you will be amazed how delicious it tastes. This would be wonderful with shrimp or sliced chicken as well.

1. Cook the gnocchi according to the package directions.

2. Place the spinach and grape tomatoes in skillet with oil and garlic, and sauté until soft, about 2–3 minutes. Add in the gnocchi and stir until well blended.

3. Place everything in large bowl. Pour pesto on top. Stir to combine. Top with Parmesan if desired.

Serves 8

1 (12-ounce) package wheat-free gnocchi
1 (6-ounce) bag organic baby spinach
1 pint of organic grape tomatoes, halved
1 teaspoon extra-virgin olive oil
1 clove garlic, chopped
Classic Pesto Sauce (see recipe in this chapter)
Fresh Parmesan cheese, for garnish (optional)

Gnocchi

Gnocchi is an Italian style potato dumpling and can be substituted for pasta in many popular dishes. Be advised, just because you hear "potato" dumplings don't assume they are wheat-free. Read your ingredient lists carefully because many of them are made with wheat flour. There are many brands that offer wheat-free gnocchi in specialty grocery stores and many local supermarkets.

Classic Pesto Sauce

Serves 8

4 ounces extra-virgin olive oil
3 cloves garlic
1½ ounces pine nuts
2 ounces freshly grated Parmesan cheese
2 ounces fresh basil leaves, torn
Salt and pepper, to taste
   (optional)

This wonderful sauce takes only a few minutes to prepare. Feel free to double this
recipe as it stores well in the freezer.

1. Add all the ingredients to a food processor
or high-speed blender in the order listed.

2. Blend for 1 minute or until blended smooth.
Depending on your blender or processor you
may need to also stir the pesto by hand to
make sure all the ingredients are combined.

Pesto Possibilities

When it comes to pesto, try thinking outside of the
box. You can substitute pine nuts with walnuts,
cashews, pistachios, almonds, or even pumpkin
seeds. To add different flavors and textures you can
also add different vegetables and cheeses. The
possibilities are endless!

Pesto, Arugula, and Yellow Tomato Pizza with Cauliflower Pizza Crust

Pizza doesn't have to consist of just cheese and sauce. It's fun to be creative with different vegetables and sauces.

1. Preheat the oven to 350°F.

2. Spread the pizza sauce evenly over the top of the cauliflower crust.

3. Spread the pesto evenly on top of the pizza sauce.

4. Sauté the arugula in a small pan with 1 tablespoon olive oil and garlic until wilted, about 1–2 minutes. Once done, pour evenly over pizza.

5. Sprinkle with the cheese, and add sliced tomatoes and fresh basil on top.

6. Bake for about 10–15 minutes, until the edges are browned.

7. Place under the broiler, on high heat, until cheese is melted, approximately 1–2 minutes.

Serves 4

2 cups Easy Pizza Sauce (see Chapter 15)
1 Cauliflower Pizza Crust (see recipe in this chapter)
½ cup Classic Pesto Sauce (see recipe in this chapter)
3 cups fresh arugula
1 tablespoon extra-virgin olive oil
1 clove garlic, minced
1 cup part-skim mozzarella cheese, shredded or fresh
1 pint of yellow cherry tomatoes, sliced in half
¼ cup freshly torn basil leaves

Cauliflower Pizza Crust

Serves 4

1 cup raw cauliflower, grated (or chopped in food processor)
1 egg
½ cup freshly grated Parmesan cheese
1 teaspoon oregano
2 teaspoons parsley
Handful of fresh basil
1 clove garlic, finely diced

Following a wheat-free diet doesn't mean you can't have pizza! This makes a 1" thick crust but it can be doubled for a larger pizza.

1. Preheat the oven to 425°F. Spray a cookie sheet with nonstick spray or use parchment paper.

2. In a medium bowl, combine the cauliflower, egg, Parmesan cheese, and all the seasonings. Press evenly on baking pan or pizza stone. Bake for 15–20 minutes, until the edges start to brown. You may turn over once if desired.

3. Remove the pan from the oven. Add sauce and desired toppings.

4. Place under the broiler, on high heat, until cheese is melted.

Cauliflower Pizza Crust Tips

Approximately 2¼ cups of cauliflower, chopped into 1" pieces, would grate into 1 cup of grated cauliflower. Be careful not to spread the crust too thin, or it will fall apart and its edges will burn. Alternatively, spreading the crust too thick will leave the middle uncooked.

Corn and Spinach Pockets Stuffed with Cheese and Artichokes

Simply because a dish is vegetarian does not mean it has to be tasteless. This recipe is a perfect example.

1. Add the defrosted artichokes to a food processor with the spinach, process and slowly add the cheeses, chives, garlic, seasonings, and egg.

2. Preheat the oven to 350°F. Lay out the crepes on a nonstick baking sheet or one covered with a sheet of aluminum foil.

3. Divide the filling among the crepes, spooning the mixture onto one half and leaving the other half plain.

4. Wet the rims of the crepes with beaten egg. Fold over and press lightly to seal, and then bake for 20 minutes or until well browned and filling is bubbling out.

Selecting and Preparing Artichokes

Look for artichokes that are tightly closed. Take a pair of kitchen scissors and clip off the sharp points. You can use a knife to cut off the tops. They are hearty when stuffed with many kinds of delicious foods. If you eat fish, salmon mixed with rice makes an excellent stuffing.

Serves 8

1 (10-ounce) box frozen artichoke hearts, thawed
1 (10-ounce) box frozen spinach, thawed, moisture squeezed out
1 cup ricotta cheese, wheat-free
4 ounces cream cheese
¼ cup minced chives
1 clove garlic, chopped
¼ teaspoon freshly ground nutmeg
Salt and pepper, to taste
1 egg
8 large (8"–9" in diameter) Corn Crepes (see Chapter 2)
Beaten egg for sealing pockets

Tofu and Vegetables with Macadamia Nuts and Asian Citrus Sauce

Serves 4

1 tablespoon sesame seed oil

3 tablespoons peanut or other vegetable oil

1 bunch scallions, chopped

1 clove garlic, minced

1" piece gingerroot, peeled and minced

⅔ pound sugar snap peas, ends trimmed

2 cups mung bean sprouts

2 cups shredded Chinese cabbage

½ teaspoon brown sugar

½ orange, juice and rind, pulsed in the food processor

1 teaspoon Asian five-spice powder, wheat-free

1 teaspoon wheat-free Chinese mustard or Japanese wasabi, or to taste

¼ cup sake or dry white wine

¼ cup light wheat-free soy sauce

1 pound satin tofu, cubed

The tastes and textures come together beautifully in this Asian-inspired dish. Serve over rice.

1. Heat the oils in a wok. Add the scallions, garlic, and gingerroot. Lightly mix in the rest of the vegetables and toss in the oil for 3–4 minutes. Place the cooked vegetables in a large, warm serving bowl.

2. In a small bowl, mix together the brown sugar, orange juice and rind, five-spice powder, mustard or wasabi, sake or wine, and soy sauce.

3. Stir into the wok until blended. Add the tofu cubes and vegetables, and mix to coat. Serve hot.

A Source of Protein for Vegetarians

Tofu, long used in Asia because meat and milk were both scarce and expensive, has become an important part of the vegetarian diet. It can be flavored to taste like many kinds of meat. Or it can be sweetened and prepared with fruit for desserts. It's delicious in soups and with vegetables.

Stuffed Portobello Mushrooms

This vegetarian dish can be prepared as an entrée with a bed of greens, or you can use smaller portobello mushrooms to make these into an appetizer.

1. Preheat the oven to 250°F.

2. Place the portobello mushrooms onto a baking sheet lined with aluminum foil.

3. Bring 3 cups of water and bouillon together to a boil.

4. Add rice, onion, tomatoes, garlic, basil, and spinach to the boiling water. Stirring occasionally, continue to boil until all the water is absorbed and the rice is fully cooked, about 15–20 minutes. Remove from heat and add the scooped-out insides of mushrooms. Stir to combine.

5. Pour rice mixture into each of the mushroom caps and top with Parmesan cheese.

6. Place mushrooms in the oven for about 20–30 minutes, or until cheese is melted.

Serves 2

2 large portobello mushrooms, stems and gills removed, wiped down with insides scooped out and set aside
3 cups water
1 teaspoon vegetable or chicken bouillon, wheat-free
1 cup brown rice, uncooked
1 medium red onion, finely chopped
¼ cup sun-dried tomatoes
3 cloves garlic, minced
¼ cup fresh basil, torn
1 cup baby spinach
½ cup fresh Parmesan cheese, grated

Classic Polenta with Herbs and Parmesan

Serves 4–6

6½ or 7 cups water
2 tablespoons salt
2 cups yellow cornmeal
2–4 ounces unsalted butter
2 cloves garlic, minced
½ medium onion, finely minced
2 tablespoons dried herbs, or 1 tablespoon each: chopped fresh basil, rosemary, and parsley
½ cup freshly grated Parmesan cheese
Freshly ground black pepper, to taste

Use 7 cups of water if you want soft polenta the consistency of mashed potatoes; use 6½ cups if you prefer it firm enough to cut into squares to broil, grill, or fry.

1. Bring the water to a boil.

2. Add salt, and using your hand to drop the cornmeal into the boiling water, let the cornmeal slip slowly between your fingers to make a very slim stream. You should be able to see each grain. Don't dump the cornmeal into the water or you will get a mass of glue.

3. Stir constantly while adding the cornmeal. Reduce heat to a simmer and keep stirring for about 20 minutes as it thickens.

4. Stir in the butter, garlic, onion, herbs, Parmesan cheese, and pepper. If you're making soft polenta, serve immediately. If you're making firm polenta, spread in a 9" × 13" lasagna pan that has been prepared with nonstick spray. Chill for 3 hours or overnight. Cut into sections and either fry, broil, or grill.

The Staple of Lombardy

Polenta has been the staple food of Lombardy, at the foot of the Italian Alps, for three centuries. Polenta is a staple in Italy, and it's hard to ruin it. You can use polenta wherever you'd use pasta, serving it with tomato, vegetable, or cream sauces, or with brown gravy and mushrooms. You can make it soft, to mound on a plate or platter, or firm and then fry it in squares.

Broccoli and Cheese-Stuffed Baked Potatoes

The whole family will love this recipe. You can experiment with variety of vegetables and different cheeses too.

1. Preheat the oven to 350°F.

2. Bake the potatoes in the oven for 40 minutes. Then cool the potatoes and split them in half lengthwise.

3. Steam broccoli until tender, about 5 minutes. Drain, rinse, and chop.

4. Spoon out the insides of the potatoes and place in a bowl; add the broccoli. Stir in the sour cream and nutmeg. Add the American cheese, garlic, and onion. Season to taste with salt and pepper.

5. Re-stuff the potato skins. Arrange the Cheddar cheese on top. Bake for another 20 minutes and serve hot.

Serves 4 as a meal, or 8 as a snack

4 large Idaho or Yukon Gold potatoes
5 cups broccoli florets
1 cup sour cream, wheat-free
¼ teaspoon nutmeg
1 cup grated white American cheese
3 cloves garlic, chopped
1 large onion, finely chopped
Salt and pepper, to taste
½ cup shredded sharp Cheddar cheese

Potato Frittata with Cheese and Herbs

Serves 4

1 large Yukon Gold potato, peeled
4 teaspoons butter
Salt and pepper to taste
6 eggs
½ cup freshly grated Parmesan cheese
½ small green onion, finely minced
1 teaspoon dried parsley
6 sage leaves, minced
Fresh herbs, extra cheese, wheat-free sour cream, for garnish

Use both nonstick spray and butter in this recipe, or the starch in the potatoes will stick. Spinach or bacon would make a lovely addition to this.

1. Using a mandoline, slice the potato as thinly as possible. Prepare a heavy 12" pan, first with nonstick spray, then with butter.

2. Add the potatoes, making a thin layer, and season with salt and pepper. Cook over medium heat for 10 minutes—this will be the crust.

3. In a large bowl, beat the eggs well. Add the cheese, onion, parsley, and minced sage. Pour over the potatoes and turn down heat to the lowest possible setting. Cook for 10 minutes.

4. When the eggs have set, run the frittata under the broiler until golden brown on top. Cut into wedges and serve at once with garnishes.

Striking Yukon Gold

Yukon Gold potatoes were developed in the 1970s at the University of Guelph, Ontario, Canada. They were initially slow to capture the market but are now widely popular, and particularly suited for baking, and for use in salads and soups.

Stuffed Eggplant with Ricotta and Spices

This dish is also known as Eggplant Sicilian. It freezes beautifully and is very delicious.

1. Stack the salted eggplant slices on a plate and put another plate with a weight on top to press the brown liquid out of them.

2. Mix the flour and pepper and use it for dredging the eggplant slices. Fry the slices in the olive oil and garlic, removing to paper towels as they are browned.

3. Preheat the oven to 325°F. Prepare a 2-quart casserole dish or a 10" × 10" glass pan with nonstick spray and spread with a thin layer of tomato sauce.

4. In a large bowl, mix the ricotta cheese, ½ cup of the Parmesan, eggs, basil, and oregano. Place a tablespoon of the egg-cheese mixture on each slice of eggplant and roll, placing seam-side down in the baking dish.

5. Spread with remaining tomato sauce, sprinkle with the rest of the Parmesan cheese and the mozzarella cheese, and bake for 35 minutes.

Smaller Is Sweeter

The smaller eggplants now available are much sweeter and not old enough to have grown bitter. Also, many have few seeds. They come in pale cream, lavender, and purple, all the way from egg-sized to long and skinny. All are good!

Serves 4

2 medium eggplants, peeled, cut in 16 round slices (8 slices each) and salted
1 cup rice or corn flour
Freshly ground black pepper, to taste
¼ cup extra-virgin olive oil, or as needed
1 clove garlic, chopped
2 cups tomato sauce
1 pound ricotta cheese, wheat-free
1 cup freshly grated Parmesan cheese, divided
2 eggs
1 teaspoon dried basil
1 tablespoon dried oregano
1 cup shredded mozzarella cheese

Classic Italian Risotto

Serves 4

5 cups canned or homemade chicken or vegetable broth, wheat-free
2 tablespoons butter
2 tablespoons extra-virgin olive oil
½ cup finely chopped sweet onion
2 cloves garlic, minced
2 stalks celery, finely chopped
¼ cup celery leaves, chopped
1½ cups arborio rice
⅓ cup dry white wine
1 teaspoon salt, or to taste
⅔ cup freshly grated Parmesan cheese
¼ cup chopped parsley
Freshly ground black pepper, to taste

Risotto should be very creamy on the outside, yet firm on the inside of each grain of rice.

1. Bring the broth to a slow simmer over low heat and keep it hot.

2. Place the butter and oil in a heavy-bottomed pot, melt butter, and add the onion, garlic, celery, and celery leaves. Cook for 8–10 minutes.

3. Add the rice and stir to coat with butter and oil. Add white wine and salt.

4. In ¼-cup increments, start adding hot broth. Stir until the broth has been absorbed into the rice. Add another ¼ cup, stirring until all of the broth is absorbed. Repeat this process until all of the hot broth is gone. It must be stirred constantly and takes about 35 minutes.

5. When all of the broth is gone, taste the rice for desired consistency. If it needs more broth or water, add it and keep stirring. Add the cheese, parsley, and pepper. Serve immediately.

Parmesan Cheese
Always grate Parmesan cheese yourself as you need it. Buy it in 1-pound blocks and keep well sealed with plastic wrap in the refrigerator. Try using a box grater for a coarse cheese with lots of body.

Vegetable Lasagna Primavera with Pasta Substitute

This vegetarian dish takes very little time and is excellent for a big family dinner or a holiday.

1. Mix 2 eggs, salt, pepper, milk or water, and corn flour in the blender and process until smooth.

2. Using a well-greased griddle, pour the batter, fry until firm, and cut into 10" strips that are 2" wide. Turn using an extra-large, long spatula. As you finish, place the strips on a baking dish that has been prepared with nonstick spray. When the bottom of the pan is covered, fry the rest of the batter in the same way and save it for topping.

3. In a bowl, mix the ricotta, other two eggs, garlic, Parmesan, vegetables, and parsley. Spread in tablespoonfuls over the base in the pan. Cover with more of the pasta strips.

4. Add the marinara sauce to the pan and cover with shredded mozzarella. Bake for about 12 minutes. Serve hot.

A Versatile Pasta

Any sauce that you would use on wheat pasta can be used on rice pasta—from a rich Alfredo sauce to a robust marinara sauce.

Serves 6–8

2 eggs
½ teaspoon table salt or sea salt, or to taste
¼ teaspoon pepper, or to taste
1½ cups milk or water
1 cup corn flour (masa harina)
Butter or oil for greasing the griddle
1 pound ricotta cheese, wheat-free
2 eggs
2 cloves garlic, chopped
½ cup Parmesan cheese, freshly grated
2 cups chopped raw mixed fresh vegetables, such as scallions, zucchini, fresh spinach, and young peas
½ cup finely chopped fresh parsley
1½ cups Spicy Marinara Sauce (see Chapter 11)
1 cup shredded mozzarella cheese

Spinach, Kale, and Mushroom Pizza

Serves 4

2 cups kale
2 cups spinach
1 cup sliced mushrooms
1 tablespoon grapeseed oil
2 cloves garlic, chopped
½ medium onion, chopped
Cauliflower Pizza Crust (see
    recipe in this chapter)
½ cup goat cheese, crumbled
Handful of fresh basil, torn

This pizza goes beyond the typical red sauce and mozzarella cheese. Goat cheese makes a wonderful addition to this sauceless pizza.

1. Place kale, spinach, and mushrooms in a skillet with grapeseed oil, garlic, and onion. Sauté for 3–4 minutes, until mushrooms soften and the greens wilt.

2. Place the vegetables on top of pizza crust. Next top with goat cheese and fresh basil.

3. Place back in the broiler for 2 minutes until cheese is melted. Serve hot.

Pizza Is a Family Affair

Making pizzas can be a fun and easy family activity. Let the kids sprinkle the cheese, add the vegetables, or tear the basil. By doing simple prep work, it's an easy way to expose "future chefs" to the joy of cooking.

Casseroles

Chapter 10

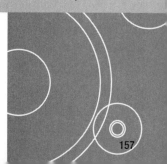

Healthy Mexican Casserole

Serves 8

1 tablespoon extra-virgin olive oil
1 pound lean ground turkey
½ teaspoon cumin
¼ teaspoon chili powder, wheat-free
¼ teaspoon red pepper flakes
⅛ teaspoon coriander
2 tablespoons water
1 (15-ounce) can black beans, rinsed thoroughly and drained
1 (15-ounce) can pinto beans, rinsed thoroughly and drained
4–5 plum tomatoes, chopped and seeds removed
1 teaspoon chopped chili peppers
½ cup frozen corn
¼ cup Mexican blend shredded cheese

This one-dish meal is so easy and delicious your family will ask you to make it again and again. Serve the casserole with Baked Corn Tortilla Chips (see Chapter 3).

1. Preheat the oven to 350°F.

2. Heat the oil in a skillet over medium-high heat. Cook turkey in hot oil for 5–8 minutes, until the meat is browned.

3. Stir in cumin, chili powder, red pepper flakes, coriander, and water.

4. Add black and pinto beans, tomatoes, chili peppers, and corn. Stir well.

5. Place the meat mixture in a 9" × 13" casserole dish and add cheese on top.

6. Bake for 20 minutes until cheese is melted.

Ditch the Packet

The packets of taco seasoning that you can find in the grocery store are loaded with sodium and preservatives. One little packet can have as much as 1,500 mg of sodium! It is easy and more economical to make your own taco seasoning blend using these simple ingredients. Plus you will ensure your seasoning blend is wheat-free!

Scalloped Potatoes with Leeks and Prosciutto

This is the ideal comfort food. It's filling and tasty and is an excellent brunch or supper dish.

1. Grease a 9" × 13" baking dish or prepare it with nonstick spray. Preheat the oven to 350°F.

2. Mix together the cheeses, corn flour, salt, and pepper.

3. Place a layer of potatoes in the baking dish, then one of leeks, and dab with bits of prosciutto. Sprinkle with the mixture of cheeses, corn flour, and spices. Repeat until you get to the top of the baking dish. Add the milk, sprinkle with cheese mixture, and dot with butter.

4. Bake for about 90 minutes. The top should be brown and crispy, the inside soft and creamy.

Serves 6

1½ cups freshly grated Parmesan cheese
1 cup coarsely grated fontina cheese
½ cup corn flour
½ teaspoon salt
½ teaspoon freshly ground pepper
6 large Idaho or Yukon Gold potatoes, peeled and sliced thinly
4 leeks, thinly sliced crosswise, white parts only
1 pound prosciutto, diced
3 cups milk
4 tablespoons butter (for greasing baking dish and dotting on potatoes)

Zucchini with Tomato and Bacon

Serves 6

6 medium zucchini
1 small onion, peeled and minced
2 cloves garlic, peeled and minced
1 serrano pepper, cored, seeded, and minced
2 tablespoons butter or extra-virgin olive oil
1 cup cooked rice
1 cup crushed tomatoes
2 tablespoons freshly squeezed lemon juice
2 eggs, slightly beaten
1 tablespoon dried oregano leaves or 2 tablespoons fresh oregano
½ teaspoon salt
½ teaspoon pepper
6 strips bacon, wheat-free

This recipe is best when made with medium-sized zucchini, about 10"–12" each, and can also easily be made vegetarian by omitting the bacon.

1. Preheat the oven to 350°F. Spray a 9" × 13" baking dish with nonstick spray or oil.

2. Cut the top quarter off the zucchini, lengthwise. Hollow out the zucchini with the small side of a melon baller or with a half-teaspoon measuring spoon; reserve the pulp.

3. In a skillet over medium heat, sauté the onion, garlic, pepper, and zucchini pulp in the butter until soft, about 3–4 minutes. Add all the remaining ingredients except the bacon.

4. Divide the filling among the zucchini boats. Lay a bacon strip on top of each stuffed zucchini. Place in the prepared baking dish. Bake until the "boats" are hot and the bacon is brown and crisp, about 10–12 minutes. Serve hot or at room temperature.

Stuffed Vegetables

There are many vegetables you can successfully stuff with lots of different, delicious ingredients. Chopped meat, shrimp, fish, and crabmeat all make wonderful stuffing. A baked clam–stuffed mushroom is also a real treat. Ricotta cheese, used to stuff pastas such as ravioli and lasagna, also makes an excellent stuffing.

Thick and Creamy Corn and Black Bean Casserole

This makes a satisfying meal and can be kept vegetarian, or add some ham for extra flavor. Feel free to substitute half-and-half for the whipping cream to lighten it up.

1. Preheat the oven to 350°F.

2. Melt the butter in a large ovenproof casserole. Add the onion, celery, celeriac, and red pepper and sauté over low heat until soft, about 10 minutes.

3. Mix in the corn flour or starch and stir, cooking gently for 3 minutes.

4. Add the chicken broth, black beans, and corn. Bring to a boil, and then lower the heat to a simmer and cook until the black beans are slightly softened, about 20 minutes. Take off the heat.

5. In a small bowl, mix together the eggs and cream. Blend the mixture quickly into the vegetables. Mix in the salt and spices.

6. Place in a well-buttered casserole or keep in the same ovenproof pan that you've been using for cooking. Sprinkle the top with bread crumbs and cheese.

7. Bake until golden brown and bubbling, about 15 minutes. Serve hot.

Serves 4–5

2 tablespoons unsalted butter
½ sweet onion, chopped fine
½ cup minced celery
½ cup minced celeriac (celery root)
¼ cup sweet red pepper, roasted and chopped
2 tablespoons corn flour, potato flour, or cornstarch
½ cup rich chicken broth, wheat-free
1 (15-ounce) can black beans, thoroughly rinsed and drained
1 (10-ounce) package frozen corn kernels
2 eggs, well beaten
1½ cups whipping cream
1 teaspoon salt
1 teaspoon sweet paprika, wheat-free
1 teaspoon ground black pepper
1 teaspoon ground coriander
½ teaspoon ground allspice, wheat-free
1 cup wheat-free bread crumbs
1 cup grated Cheddar cheese

Better Than Canned
Stay away from canned creamed corn and stick with fresh or frozen, making your own cream sauce. It's easy and wheat-free, and tastes so much better than the ones made with soups or mixes.

Chicken Divan

Serves 6

3 pounds chicken breasts,
   boneless and skinless, cut
   into strips
1 cup corn flour
1 tablespoon sea or kosher salt
Ground black pepper, to taste
½ cup extra-virgin olive oil, or
   more as needed
1 pound broccoli florets, cut into
   bite-sized pieces, cooked,
   and drained
1½ cups Incredible Hollandaise
   Sauce (see Chapter 11)
2 tablespoons freshly grated
   Parmesan cheese
Sprinkle of paprika, wheat-free
   (optional)

Chicken lovers will be asking for second helpings when they try this mouthwatering dish.

1. Preheat the oven to 350°F.

2. Roll the chicken in the flour, sprinkle with salt and pepper.

3. Heat the olive oil in a sauté pan over medium heat. Sauté the chicken for 5 minutes on each side until golden brown, adding more oil if the pan gets dry.

4. Butter a 2-quart casserole or prepare it with nonstick spray. Place the broccoli in the bottom and spoon some Hollandaise over the top. Arrange the chicken over the broccoli and pour on the rest of the sauce. Sprinkle with Parmesan cheese and paprika. Bake for 30 minutes.

Red Rice and Sausage

This is so easy—and perfect for when you are low on time. Kids love it and grown-ups do too.

1. Brown the sausage pieces, onion, and garlic in oven-safe skillet over medium-high heat for 5–8 minutes. If the sausage is very lean, add a bit of olive oil to prevent the food from sticking.

2. Stir in the rice and toss with the sausage and vegetables. Add the broth and rosemary and cover. Cook on very low heat or place in a 325°F oven for 45–60 minutes.

3. Just before serving, sprinkle the top with Parmesan cheese and brown under the broiler. Add the chopped parsley and serve.

What Is Red Rice?

Yes there is more out there than white or brown rice! Red rice is often found in Europe, Southeast Asia, and India. Red rice has similar nutritional information as brown rice, as they are both high in fiber. When red rice is cooked, the natural red color of the bran leaches out and turns the rest of the rice a reddish-pink color.

Serves 4–6

1 pound sweet or hot Italian sausage, wheat-free, cut into 1" pieces

1 medium onion, finely chopped

2 cloves garlic, chopped

1 cup red rice, uncooked

2¾ cups chicken broth, wheat-free

1 teaspoon dried rosemary or 1 tablespoon fresh rosemary

½ cup freshly grated Parmesan cheese

¼ cup chopped fresh parsley

Tuscan Bean, Tomato, and Parmesan Casserole

Serves 4–6

4 slices bacon, wheat-free
¼ cup extra-virgin olive oil
4 cloves garlic, coarsely chopped
1 medium onion, peeled and coarsely chopped
½ fresh fennel bulb, coarsely chopped
1 tablespoon rice flour
2 (15-ounce) cans white beans, drained and rinsed
16 ounces tomatoes, chopped (canned is fine)
1 medium zucchini, chopped
1 tablespoon chopped fresh basil
1 teaspoon dried oregano
1 teaspoon dried rosemary
½ cup fresh Italian parsley, rinsed and chopped
1 teaspoon dried red pepper flakes, or to taste
1 teaspoon salt, or to taste
½ cup freshly grated Parmesan cheese
2 tablespoons unsalted butter, cut into small pieces

This is fantastic comfort food. If you are looking for a satisfying, warming, and delicious meal, this is it!

1. Preheat the oven to 350°F.

2. Fry the bacon in a skillet until almost crisp. Place on paper towels to drain. Remove all but 1 teaspoon of bacon fat from pan. Chop bacon and set aside.

3. Add the oil, garlic, onion, and fennel to the skillet. Sauté over low heat for 10 minutes, or until softened but not browned.

4. Blend the flour into the mixture and cook for 3 minutes, mixing well.

5. Add the beans, tomatoes, and zucchini. Mix well and pour into a casserole dish.

6. Add the herbs, red pepper flakes, and salt, and stir. Mix in the reserved chopped bacon.

7. Sprinkle Parmesan cheese and butter over the top and bake for 25 minutes, or until the cheese is lightly browned.

Eat More Beans

There are more varieties of beans than it's possible to list here. They are delicious and loaded with protein, vitamins, minerals, and fiber. If a culture, or a household, needs to stretch its food supply, beans are the answer. They come in red and pink, green and orange, black and white, speckled or solid. Some have black eyes and others look like cranberries. Beans—legumes—are available in many sizes and shapes, from tiny peas to big kidneys.

Beef Stroganoff

This is an elegant, historic recipe, named after the Russian general who is said to have invented it. You can serve it with potato pancakes on the side, with wild rice or wheat-free pasta.

1. In a large sauté pan, heat the oil over medium heat and add the onion, mushrooms, and garlic. Cook for 5 minutes to soften.

2. Add the flour, mustard, and salt and pepper to the pan, and stir to blend.

3. Mix in the warmed beef broth, cook, and stir to thicken. Stir in the wine and Worcestershire sauce and bring to a boil. Turn off the heat.

4. On a large piece of waxed paper, roll the beef in flour.

5. Heat the unsalted butter in a separate pan. Sear the beef in the butter for 1 minute to quickly brown and seal in the juices.

6. Spoon the beef into the mushroom sauce, add the dill weed, and stir to blend. Simmer for 10–15 minutes; the beef should be medium rare.

7. Just before serving, add the sour cream. Spoon over a bed of wild rice or serve with potato pancakes on the side.

Why Not to Wash Mushrooms

Mushrooms are grown in a safe and sanitary medium that has been treated with thermophilic bacteria. This kills any germs by naturally heating the growing medium to a very high temperature. Also, washing mushrooms makes them mushy because they absorb the water. Please don't peel them, either—just brush them off.

Serves 6

2 tablespoons extra-virgin olive oil

1 medium white onion, chopped

8 ounces tiny button mushrooms, brushed clean, stems removed

2 cloves garlic, minced

2 tablespoons tapioca flour, plus ¼ cup for coating the meat

1 teaspoon dried mustard

Salt and pepper, to taste

1½ cups beef broth, wheat-free, warmed

1 cup dry red wine

1 teaspoon wheat-free Worcestershire sauce

2 pounds filet mignon, cut into bite-sized cubes

2 tablespoons unsalted butter

2 tablespoons snipped fresh dill weed

1 cup wheat-free sour cream or crème fraîche

Tuna-Noodle Casserole

Serves 6

8 ounces brown rice noodles
1 tablespoon butter
½ medium onion, finely
   chopped
2 large carrots, finely chopped
1 red bell pepper, sliced
1 clove garlic, minced
1½ cups milk
1 cup chicken broth, wheat-free
½ teaspoon marjoram
3 tablespoons cornstarch
½ teaspoon salt
1 teaspoon pepper
2 (6-ounce) cans white alba-
   core tuna, drained and flaked
1 cup shredded sharp Cheddar
   cheese
2 tablespoons Asiago cheese

This creamy, kid-friendly dish is simple to make and can be a wonderful lunch or dinner.

1. Preheat the oven to 375°F. Spray a 9" × 13" baking dish with nonstick cooking spray.

2. Bring a large pot of lightly salted water to a boil. Add noodles, cook for 6–8 minutes, until al dente, and drain.

3. Melt the butter in a skillet over medium-low heat. Stir in the onion, carrots, red pepper, and garlic, and cook for 5 minutes, until tender.

4. Increase the heat to medium-high, and continue to cook and stir for 5 minutes, or until most of the liquid has evaporated.

5. In a medium-sized saucepan, mix the milk, broth, marjoram, and cornstarch and stir until thoroughly mixed. Cook over medium heat for 5 minutes, until the sauce is smooth and slightly thickened. Season with salt and pepper.

6. Stir in the tuna, carrot mixture, cooked noodles, and Cheddar cheese. Transfer to the prepared baking dish.

7. Bake for 25 minutes, or until bubbly and lightly browned. Top with Asiago cheese.

Baked Mushroom and Fontina Risotto

You can add so many other ingredients to this recipe—cubes of cooked chicken or turkey, chopped pears or apples, and your favorite herbs.

1. Preheat the oven to 350°F.

2. Heat 1 tablespoon butter and the olive oil in an ovenproof casserole. Sauté the onion and garlic over a low flame until softened, about 2–3 minutes.

3. Add the salt, pepper, oregano, sage, and rice. Stir to coat the rice. Add the broth and vermouth. Cover the dish and place in the oven.

4. After the rice has cooked for 20 minutes, heat the remaining butter in a skillet and sauté the mushrooms for 3–4 minutes.

5. Stir the mushroom/butter mixture into the rice. Re-cover the casserole and continue to cook for 15 minutes.

6. Just before serving, stir in the fontina cheese.

A Misunderstood Italian Staple

Most cooks think that risotto is simply rice that has been boiled with broth and herbs. But it's so much more—the technique for making risotto is simple but demanding. The secret is the rice and how it's slow cooked, using a bit of liquid until it's absorbed and then a bit more. It's been said that the rice will tell you when to add liquid—it hisses and sizzles, asking for the broth!

Serves 6–8

3 tablespoon butter, divided
3 tablespoons extra-virgin olive oil
1 small onion, minced
2 cloves garlic, minced
½ teaspoon salt
½ teaspoon pepper
½ teaspoon ground oregano
6 large leaves fresh sage, ripped or cut up, or 2 teaspoons dried sage, crumbled
1 cup long grain rice
2½ cups chicken broth, wheat-free
½ cup white vermouth
8 ounces mixed mushrooms (shiitake, porcini, morels, chanterelles)
⅓ cup grated fontina cheese

Egg and Turkey Sausage Casserole

Serves 6

1 tablespoon extra-virgin olive oil
1 (16-ounce) package lean turkey breakfast sausage, wheat-free
2 cups baby spinach, rinsed and dried
¼ cup shredded Cheddar cheese
6 whole eggs
6 egg whites
½ cup skim milk

This healthy and simple dish is perfect to make the night before for brunch or breakfast. Feel free to experiment with different types of vegetables and cheeses too.

1. Spray a 9" × 13" casserole dish with cooking spray to prevent sticking. Preheat the oven to 350°F.

2. In a large skillet, heat oil over medium-high heat. Cook breakfast sausage for about 5–7 minutes, or until no longer pink inside. Place on a plate covered with paper towels to drain. Let cool, then cut into 1" slices.

3. Place the spinach on the bottom of casserole dish. Top with sausage slices and sprinkle shredded cheese on top.

4. In a large bowl, whisk eggs and egg whites with milk. Continue to beat until frothy.

5. Pour egg and milk mixture over casserole and bake for 35 minutes until completely set.

Enchilada Casserole

This is definitely a crowd pleaser. You can adjust the spices according to your guests' tastes.

1. Preheat the oven to 425°F.

2. Heat oil in a very large, deep skillet or Dutch oven and cook onion and garlic for 3–4 minutes until they soften.

3. Add the ground beef, chili powder, cumin, cayenne pepper, and cilantro and cook for 5–8 minutes, until beef turns brown.

4. Add the beans, tomatoes, green pepper, carrot, chili peppers, and corn. Season with salt and cook additional 1–2 minutes until thoroughly combined.

5. Spray a 9" × 13" casserole dish with non-stick cooking spray. Layer the corn tortillas, then meat mixture, then cheese. Repeat again until all ingredients are used.

6. Bake for 15 minutes until the cheese is melted. Top with scallion, avocado, sour cream, olives, and salsa.

Serves 6

2 tablespoons extra-virgin olive oil
½ medium onion, chopped
1 clove garlic, minced
2 pounds lean ground beef
1 tablespoon chili powder, wheat-free
1 tablespoon cumin
⅛ teaspoon cayenne pepper, ground, wheat-free
1 tablespoon chopped fresh cilantro
1 (15-ounce) can black or pinto beans, thoroughly rinsed and drained
1 cup diced tomatoes or 1 (14-ounce) can diced tomatoes
½ cup green pepper, diced
1 large carrot, shredded
1 can diced green chili peppers
1 cup frozen corn
¼ teaspoon salt
8–12 corn tortillas, wheat-free, amount depends on how many you want to use
2 cups sharp Cheddar or Monterey jack cheese, shredded
2 scallions, finely chopped
1 avocado, peeled, pitted, and sliced
1 cup sour cream, wheat-free
½ cup sliced black olives
1 cup wheat-free salsa

Eggplant Parmesan

Serves 10

2 medium eggplants, peeled
and thinly sliced
1 teaspoon sea salt
3 large eggs, plus 2 egg whites,
lightly beaten
2 cups wheat-free bread
crumbs
¾ cup ground flaxseed
1 teaspoon oregano
4 cloves garlic, minced
½ cup freshly grated Parmesan
cheese, divided
6 cups Easy Pizza Sauce (see
Chapter 15) or wheat-free
spaghetti sauce
2 cups mozzarella cheese,
shredded
1 tablespoon fresh basil

This popular Italian dish is transformed into an easy, healthy casserole.

1. Preheat the oven to 350°F.

2. Slice eggplant and place in 9" × 13" casserole dish. Add salt to eggplant and let sit for 1 hour to let eggplant "sweat" out extra moisture. After the hour, put eggplant in colander and rinse excess salt off. Pat dry with paper towels.

3. Place beaten eggs in shallow bowl.

4. In another shallow bowl, add the bread crumbs, flaxseed, oregano, garlic, and ¼ cup Parmesan cheese. Stir well to combine.

5. Spray a baking sheet with nonstick cooking spray. Dip eggplant in egg, then bread crumb mixture and place onto baking sheet. Bake for 10 minutes on each side.

6. Spread ½–¾ cup pizza sauce on the bottom of the casserole dish. Place a layer of eggplant on top of sauce layer. Sprinkle with Parmesan and ½ cup–¾ cup mozzarella cheeses. Repeat another layer of sauce, eggplant, and cheese until ingredients run out.

7. Top with fresh basil. Bake for 20 minutes or until golden brown and cheese is melted.

Why Do You Need to "Sweat" Out Eggplant?

Eggplants can be very bitter. Once you remove moisture from it, the eggplant will become less bitter. The salt helps remove the moisture from the eggplant. Just be sure to rinse it thoroughly so it isn't too salty.

Pasta and Sauces

Chapter 11

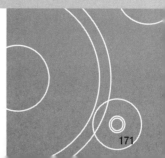

Asparagus, Mushrooms, and Yellow Tomatoes with Brown Rice Pasta

Serves 6

1 (16-ounce) package of brown rice pasta
1 tablespoon extra-virgin olive oil
2 cloves garlic, chopped
1 pound fresh asparagus, cut in half
1 pint yellow tomatoes, sliced in half
1 organic yellow pepper, sliced in strips
1 organic orange pepper, sliced in strips
1 cup mushrooms, sliced
½ cup vegetable broth (or broth of your choice), wheat-free
1 tablespoon fresh Parmesan cheese, grated
Salt and pepper, to taste

Fresh vegetables work best in this dish. This dish is packed with flavor and full of color.

1. Prepare the brown rice pasta according to the instructions on the package. This pasta should be prepared al dente. Rinse thoroughly with cool water to stop the cooking process and drain.

2. Place the oil, garlic, and vegetables in a skillet and sauté for 3–4 minutes, until they soften. Add vegetable broth and stir until well blended. Let cook for another 2–3 minutes, until the vegetables are tender.

3. Place the vegetables on top of the brown rice pasta and top with freshly shaved Parmesan cheese. Season with salt and pepper to taste.

Brown Rice Pasta

Make sure you cook your brown rice pasta according to the instructions. If it is overcooked, it becomes mushy and hardly palatable. If it is undercooked, it becomes chewy. It may take a few times to get the perfect, al dente brown rice pasta.

Sun-Dried Tomato–Artichoke Pasta with White Beans

Although this dish is vegetarian, cooked chicken or sausage would be a nice addition.

1. Place the oil and garlic in large skillet and let simmer for 1–2 minutes, until the garlic softens.

2. Add the sun-dried tomatoes, mushrooms, artichoke hearts, and beans, and let simmer for 3–4 minutes, until they soften.

3. Add broth and let simmer for 3–4 minutes. Add arugula, mix well, and remove from heat. You do not want the arugula to get too soft.

4. Cook the brown rice pasta according to instructions. Rinse pasta with cool water and drain.

5. Mix pasta with broth and veggie mixture. Top with shaved Parmesan if desired.

Serves 6

1 tablespoon grapeseed oil
3 cloves garlic, finely chopped
1 cup sun-dried tomatoes, sliced
2 cups chopped mushrooms
1 (9-ounce) box frozen artichoke hearts, rinsed and drained
1 (15-ounce) can small white beans, rinsed thoroughly and drained
2 cups vegetable broth, wheat-free
3 cups arugula
1 (16-ounce) package brown rice pasta
2 tablespoons fresh shaved Parmesan cheese (optional)

Corn Pasta in Rich Cream Sauce with Prosciutto, Gorgonzola, and Walnuts

Makes 2½ cups

1 (10-ounce) package corn pasta
3 tablespoons unsalted butter
3 tablespoons corn flour
2 cups medium cream, warmed
2 tablespoons minced prosciutto
½ cup crumbled Gorgonzola or blue cheese
¼ teaspoon ground nutmeg
½ cup walnut pieces, toasted
Salt and pepper, to taste

This is a delicious variation on the basic cream sauce. Feel free to lighten this up using half-and-half instead of the cream.

1. Cook corn pasta according to instructions on the package.

2. Melt the butter in a large skillet and stir in the flour. Sauté, stirring for 4–5 minutes over medium-low heat. Add the warm cream, whisking constantly until thickened to desired consistency.

3. Remove from the heat and stir in the prosciutto, cheese, nutmeg, walnuts, and salt and pepper. Serve immediately.

Rich Cream Sauces Are Versatile

You can add herbs, stock, or even bacon to a rich cream sauce. You can add cheese such as mascarpone or some prosciutto. The addition of mushrooms adds body and flavor too! You can adapt a cream sauce to loads of fish, meat, and vegetable dishes and benefit from the lush flavors.

Rice Pasta in Spicy Spinach and Lobster Sauce

Rice pasta is found in Asian markets and some specialty supermarkets.

1. Cook rice pasta according to instructions.

2. Plunge the lobster into plenty of boiling salted water. Cook for 15 minutes. Cool; crack the shell and remove the meat. Set the meat aside.

3. In a large saucepan, melt the butter and add the cornstarch, stirring until smooth. Whisk in the broth. Add the cream and heat.

4. Stir in the spinach and cook until wilted. Add the sherry, nutmeg, red pepper flakes, and reserved lobster. Sprinkle with salt and pepper. Serve over the rice pasta.

Serves 4

1 (16-ounce) package rice pasta
1 (1½-pound) lobster
2 tablespoons butter
2 tablespoons cornstarch
1 cup hot chicken or clam broth, wheat-free
1 cup heavy cream
3 cups fresh baby spinach, rinsed and stems trimmed
1 tablespoon dry sherry
Pinch ground nutmeg
1 teaspoon hot red pepper flakes or cayenne pepper, wheat-free
Salt and pepper, to taste

Carbonara Sauce

Makes 1½ cups

4 strips bacon, wheat-free
4 shallots, minced
2 teaspoons coarsely ground
  black pepper
1 cup heavy cream
2 eggs, beaten
½ cup freshly grated Parmesan
  cheese
¼ cup chopped fresh parsley
1 tablespoon fresh rosemary, or
  1 teaspoon dried, crumbled
1 teaspoon cracked black peppercorns, or to taste

This is not for someone on a diet; however, it's very delicious and easy to make. You can lighten this up by using half-and-half instead of heavy cream and cut the cheese to ¼ cup.

1. Cook the bacon over low heat until it is fried crisp, then remove it to paper towels to drain. Let it cool and crumble it. Reserve the fat.

2. Sauté the shallots in the bacon fat. Add the black pepper and cream. Bring to a boil and cook over medium-low heat until thick, about 4–5 minutes.

3. In a medium bowl, mix the eggs and cheese. Whisk in a tablespoon of sauce. Continue to add sauce slowly, whisking constantly. Add the parsley, crumbled rosemary, crumbled bacon, and peppercorns.

4. Pour over rice noodles, quinoa pasta, or spaghetti squash. (You probably won't need salt because there's salt in the bacon.)

Carbonara Fan

The origins of carbonara are found in Italy, but whether it comes from Rome or the Lazio region is uncertain. Food writer Calvin Trillin, author of *The Tummy Trilogy*, is such a fan of carbonara sauce that he suggested it replace turkey as the American holiday dish on Thanksgiving Day.

Zucchini Pasta with Parmesan and Spicy Marinara Sauce

This is such a fun substitution for regular noodles or pasta. This dish is also a perfect way to get more vegetables into your diet.

1. Cut the zucchini into thin, noodle-like strips using a peeler or mandoline.

2. Heat the oil in a large skillet over medium-high heat. Add zucchini and garlic; cook and stir until just tender, about 5 minutes. Season to taste with salt and pepper.

3. Sprinkle with Parmesan cheese. Top with Spicy Marinara Sauce.

Serves 4

4 large zucchini
1 tablespoon grapeseed oil
2–3 cloves garlic, minced
Salt and black pepper, to taste
3 tablespoons fresh Parmesan cheese, grated
Spicy Marinara Sauce (see recipe in this chapter)

Spicy Marinara Sauce

Serves 10

3 tablespoons extra-virgin
   olive oil
1 medium onion, finely chopped
6 cloves garlic, minced
1 teaspoon oregano, dried
1 teaspoon parsley, dried
¾ teaspoon rosemary, dried
1 cup fresh basil leaves, torn
¾ teaspoon marjoram
½ teaspoon crushed red pepper
   flakes
2 (28-ounce) cans crushed
   tomatoes
1 red bell pepper, seeded and
   finely chopped
½ cup dry white wine
Salt and pepper, to taste

This sauce is perfect for many dishes. You
can adjust the spiciness by increasing or
decreasing the red pepper flakes.

1. Heat the olive oil in a large pan. Add onion
and spices. Cover and cook for 10 minutes.

2. Add all other ingredients and simmer gently
for 75 minutes.

Spaghetti Squash with Creamy Vodka and Shrimp Sauce

The squash can be prepared a day in advance. Spaghetti squash is extremely versatile and tastes wonderful in many sauces, from a tomato-filled marinara to a meaty Bolognese.

1. Place the cooked squash in a large bowl and keep warm while you make the sauce.

2. Sauté the minced shallots and garlic in a mixture of oil and butter in a large skillet for 2–3 minutes. When soft, add the cornstarch. Cook and stir over low heat until well blended, for 3–4 minutes.

3. Add the vodka and tomatoes. Cover and simmer gently for 20 minutes.

4. Stir in the cream and heat slowly, then add the shrimp. Do not boil after the cream has been added. When the shrimp turns pink, about 2–3 minutes, pour over the spaghetti squash, and add salt and pepper to taste. Garnish with parsley, basil, and prosciutto.

Serves 6

1 large (4–5 pounds) spaghetti squash, cooked

2 minced shallots

1 clove garlic, minced

2 tablespoons extra-virgin olive oil

1 tablespoon butter

1 tablespoon cornstarch

½ cup vodka

1 (28-ounce) can crushed tomatoes

1 cup heavy cream

1½ pounds shrimp, peeled and deveined

Salt and plenty of freshly ground pepper, to taste

½ cup each chopped fresh parsley and basil

¼ cup prosciutto, minced, for garnish

Greek Eggplant and Olive Sauce

Serves 4

2 tablespoons flax meal
½ cup rice flour mixed with 1
    teaspoon salt
1 medium eggplant, peeled and
    cubed
⅓ cup extra-virgin olive oil
2 cloves garlic, minced
½ cup kalamata or other black,
    Greek olives, pitted and
    chopped
10 mint leaves, coarsely
    chopped
½ cup finely snipped chives
Juice of ½ lemon
Extra olive oil if sauce seems
    dry

Here you have many of the flavors of Greece without the travel. Touches of garlic and mint do not overwhelm. Goes great over wheat-free pasta or rice.

1. Mix the ground flax with the flour and salt. Dredge the eggplant cubes in flour mixture.

2. In a saucepan, heat the olive oil over medium-high heat. Sauté the eggplant until brown.

3. When brown, lower heat and add the garlic; sauté for another 3 minutes.

4. Add the rest of the ingredients and serve.

Confetti and Rice Pasta with Chicken

This is fun to eat and pretty to look at. The "confetti" is minced vegetables. Lots of Parmesan cheese completes the dish.

1. In a large skillet over medium heat, heat the olive oil and add the pepper, squash, scallions, and garlic. Sauté, stirring frequently for 3–4 more minutes.

2. While the vegetables are sautéing, mix the flour, salt, pepper, and thyme on a piece of waxed paper.

3. Dredge the chicken in the flour mixture and add to the pan along with the vegetables.

4. Add the broth, tomatoes, oregano, basil, and plenty of red pepper flakes. Cook, uncovered, for 10 minutes to make sure the chicken is done.

5. Add the rice pasta to the pan of sauce and mix. Sprinkle with plenty of Parmesan cheese and serve.

Rice Pasta

Rice pasta is available online and at Asian markets. Many supermarkets also carry it. Soba—Japanese noodles—have both buckwheat flour and wheat flour in them and sometimes the contents are listed in Japanese characters.

Serves 4

½ cup extra-virgin olive oil
½ cup finely chopped sweet red pepper
½ cup finely chopped yellow summer squash
½ cup zucchini squash, finely chopped
1 bunch scallions, chopped fine
2 cloves garlic, chopped fine
½ cup rice or corn flour
1 teaspoon salt
½ teaspoon pepper, or to taste
½ teaspoon dried thyme
¾ pound boneless, skinless chicken breast, cut into bite-sized pieces
½ cup chicken broth, wheat-free
8 ripe plum (Roma) tomatoes, chopped, or 1½ cups canned
1 teaspoon dried oregano
1 teaspoon dried basil
1 tablespoon red pepper flakes, or to taste
1 pound rice pasta, cooked
1 cup freshly grated Parmesan cheese

Spring Vegetables with Pesto and Pasta

Serves 4

½ medium onion, sliced
1 tablespoon extra-virgin olive
    oil
1 bunch asparagus, trimmed
    and cut into 1" pieces
3 large carrots, peeled and
    sliced
1 cup arugula
½ cup shelled English peas
Wheat-free pasta of your choice
Classic Pesto Sauce (see
    Chapter 9)

This dish is so easy to prepare and tastes wonderful with grilled chicken, shrimp, or steak.

1. Place the onion in a large skillet with oil. Sauté until translucent, about 3–4 minutes.

2. Add asparagus and carrots. Let cook for 5 minutes, until their colors brighten and they become tender.

3. Add arugula and peas, and stir to combine for 1 minute until arugula wilts. Remove from heat and place in a large bowl.

4. Cook pasta according to instructions. When finished cooking, toss vegetables and pasta together. Add the amount of pesto to your liking.

Quinoa Angel Hair with Bolognese Sauce

Quinoa pasta has become more popular for its added protein and wonderful texture. Most grocery stores and specialty markets carry quinoa pasta. If you can't find it, feel free to substitute another wheat-free pasta or rice.

1. In a large skillet over medium heat, place the oil, garlic, and onion. Sauté for 3–4 minutes, until onions are translucent and tender.

2. Add the ground beef, pancetta, and ground pork and brown over medium heat until no longer pink, about 5–8 minutes.

3. Once the meat is cooked, add mushrooms and carrots and cook for 3–4 minutes, until they soften.

4. Add Spicy Marinara Sauce (you can adjust the spices, when preparing the Spicy Marinara Sauce, according to your tastes) and let simmer over low heat for 20–25 minutes, stirring occasionally.

5. Cook quinoa angel hair pasta according to instructions. Place Bolognese sauce on top. Add grated Parmesan cheese if desired.

Serves 4–6

1 tablespoon extra-virgin olive oil
2 cloves garlic, chopped
½ medium onion, chopped
1 pound lean ground beef, turkey, or chicken
2 ounces diced pancetta, wheat-free
½ cup lean ground pork
½ cup chopped mushrooms
½ cup chopped carrots
Spicy Marinara Sauce (see recipe in this chapter)
1 (8-ounce) package quinoa angel hair pasta
Fresh Parmesan cheese, for topping (optional)

Pasta Primavera with Summer Vegetables

Serves 6

16 ounces wheat-free pasta of your choice

3 tablespoons extra-virgin olive oil

½ green onion, chopped

2 cloves garlic, minced

1 large carrot, peeled and diced

1 large zucchini, peeled and diced

1 summer squash, peeled and diced

½ medium green bell pepper, seeded and diced

½ medium red bell pepper, seeded and diced

½ cup chopped green beans

½ small eggplant, sliced into ¼" slices, peeled and cut crosswise

½ cup sliced plum tomatoes

½ cup Spicy Marinara Sauce (see recipe in this chapter)

Freshly grated Parmesan cheese, for topping (optional)

Salt and pepper, to taste

This dish can be served over brown rice pasta, quinoa pasta, rice, or even quinoa. Feel free to add some shrimp or chicken to it if you'd like.

1. Cook pasta according to package instructions. Rinse with cool water and set aside.

2. In a large skillet over medium heat, add the oil, onion, and garlic. Cook for 2–3 minutes, until onions and garlic become tender.

3. Add the vegetables and stir to combine. Cook vegetables about 10 minutes, until they soften. Remove from heat.

4. Add the marinara sauce to the vegetables and stir to combine. Add pasta and stir once again. Top with grated Parmesan cheese and salt and pepper to taste if desired.

Shrimp Fra Diavolo

This dish is spicy, but you can easily adjust the spices according to your taste.

1. In a large skillet over medium heat, heat oil, garlic, and onion. Cook for 3–4 minutes, until tender and aromatic.

2. Add the tomatoes, basil, oregano, white wine, salt, and red pepper flakes. Lower heat and cook 25 minutes, stirring occasionally.

3. Add shrimp to tomato mixture and cook 5–8 minutes, until cooked through.

4. Pour shrimp sauce over cooked pasta. Top with chopped parsley.

Fra Diavolo

Fra Diavolo means "brother devil" in Italian, named for its spicy taste. If you like it even spicier, increase the red pepper flakes to 1 teaspoon. You can also use any type of shellfish in this dish for variety.

Serves 6

2 tablespoons extra-virgin olive oil
6 cloves garlic, chopped
½ medium onion, minced
4 medium tomatoes, chopped
1 tablespoon ground basil
1 tablespoon ground oregano
½ cup dry white wine
1 teaspoon salt
½ teaspoon crushed red pepper flakes
16 ounces small shrimp, peeled and deveined
½ pound wheat-free pasta of choice, cooked according to instructions
1 tablespoon fresh parsley, chopped

Pasta and Sausage in Garlic–White Wine Sauce

Serves 6

1 pound wheat-free pasta of
　your choice
3 cloves garlic, minced
2 tablespoons extra-virgin olive
　oil, divided
1 pound asparagus, ends
　trimmed and cut into ¼"
　pieces
1 pint organic grape tomatoes,
　halved
1 (8-ounce) package mush-
　rooms, cleaned and sliced
1 (6-ounce) package baby
　spinach
1 tablespoon oregano, dried
1 teaspoon rosemary
1 tablespoon basil, dried
Pinch of salt and pepper
½ cup dry white wine
½ cup low-sodium chicken
　stock, wheat-free
1 (16-ounce) package pork
　sausage (you can also use
　turkey or chicken sausage),
　wheat-free
1 tablespoon fresh Parmesan
　cheese, shaved

This light, simple dish is loaded with flavor.
Vermouth is a perfect substitution for dry
white wine if you don't have any.

1. Cook pasta according to instructions.

2. Place minced garlic and 1 tablespoon of
olive oil in large skillet and let simmer for 1–2
minutes over medium-low heat.

3. Add chopped asparagus, tomatoes, and
mushrooms and cook for 3–4 minutes until
they get tender.

4. Add baby spinach and cook 2–3 more minutes until spinach is soft. Sprinkle with seasonings and stir until well blended.

5. Add wine and chicken stock, stir, and lower
heat. Let simmer for 3–4 minutes.

6. While the veggies are simmering, take out
a grill pan. In remaining 1 tablespoon olive oil,
grill sausages until no longer pink. Remove
casings if you like.

7. Add vegetable mixture to cooked
pasta. Add sliced sausage and stir until well
blended. Sprinkle Parmesan cheese on top.

Creamy Cheddar Sauce with Ham and Sherry

This is excellent over vegetables, spaghetti squash, or rice. You can also use prosciutto if you don't have smoked ham.

1. In a skillet over medium-low heat, melt the butter and stir in the flour. Sauté, stirring for 4–5 minutes.

2. Add the warm milk or cream, whisking constantly, until thickened to desired consistency, about 3–5 minutes.

3. Remove from the heat and stir in the cheese, ham, sherry, salt, and pepper. Serve.

Sherry as a Flavoring
There are several kinds of sherry used in cooking, including dry and sweet varieties. Sweet sherry is often called cream sherry, as in Harvey's Bristol Cream. Really good sherry is made in Spain by British companies who export it all over the world. The Chinese love it in sauces and soups, and it does add a wonderful flavor. It's also good in shrimp bisque, lobster Newburg, and other seafood dishes.

Makes 2½ cups

3 tablespoons unsalted butter
3 tablespoons corn flour
2 cups milk or cream, warmed
⅔ cup grated sharp Cheddar cheese
¼ cup minced smoked ham
2 teaspoons sherry
Salt and pepper, to taste

Roasted Garlic Sauce with Cheese

Makes ¾ cup

1 head garlic unpeeled, dampened
3 teaspoons unsalted butter
1 teaspoon cornstarch
½ cup milk
¼ cup chicken broth, wheat-free
2 tablespoons minced Italian
  flat-leaf parsley
2 tablespoons extra-virgin
  olive oil
1 teaspoon wheat-free vinegar
  or lemon juice
Salt and pepper, to taste
2 tablespoons fresh Parmesan
  cheese, grated

If you haven't tried roasted garlic yet, now is the time! Roasting garlic is simple and makes the garlic milder, softer, and sweeter.

1. Preheat the oven to 300°F.

2. Wrap the dampened garlic in aluminum foil and roast in oven for 60 minutes. Cool until you can handle it. Cut off the tip ends and squeeze garlic out of the shells; set aside.

3. In a saucepan, melt butter over low heat and stir in the cornstarch. Continue to cook for 3–4 minutes over low heat. Whisk in the milk, chicken broth, parsley, and olive oil.

4. Add vinegar or lemon juice, salt, pepper, cheese, and reserved garlic.

5. Place mixture in the blender and process until smooth. Pour into a serving bowl and use with vegetables, spaghetti squash, salads, rice, or tomatoes.

Incredible Hollandaise Sauce

This sauce is so adaptable and can be used on fish, lobster, or hot vegetables, especially asparagus, artichokes, and broccoli.

1. Melt the butter in a small, heavy saucepan over very low heat.

2. Place the eggs, egg yolks, lemon juice, and cayenne in a blender or food processor. Blend well.

3. With the motor running on low, add the hot butter, a little at a time, to the egg mixture.

4. Return the mixture to the pan you used to melt the butter. Whisking, thicken the sauce over low heat, adding salt to your taste, about 5–7 minutes. As soon as it's thick, pour the sauce into a bowl, a sauce boat, or over the food. (Reheating the sauce to thicken it is the delicate part. You must not let it get too hot or it will scramble the eggs, or even curdle them. If either disaster happens, add a tablespoon of boiling water and whisk vigorously.)

Hollandaise Sauce

The name implies that this sauce was created in Holland, a land of high butter use. However, it is one of the five master sauces in French cuisine. It is believed to have been created by French chefs to mimic a Dutch sauce. But in any area where there is plentiful butter, Hollandaise sauce, with its rich, smooth texture, will reign. And although people tend to think of it in terms of eggs Benedict, it's good on most green vegetables.

Makes 1¼ cups

2 sticks (1 cup) unsalted butter
1 whole egg, plus 1 or 2 egg yolks, depending on the richness desired
1 tablespoon freshly squeezed lemon juice
⅛ teaspoon cayenne pepper, wheat-free
Salt, to taste

Creamy Pesto Dipping Sauce

Serves 10–12

4 ounces extra-virgin olive oil

3 cloves garlic

1½ ounces pine nuts

2 ounces freshly grated Parmesan cheese

2 ounces fresh basil leaves, torn

4 ounces half-and-half

This sauce is perfect for dipping chicken or other meat in, or use on top of wheat-free pasta.

1. Add all the ingredients to food processor or high-powered blender in the order listed.

2. Blend for 2–3 minutes, until smooth. Serve immediately, or store in the refrigerator until ready to serve.

Simple Zucchini-Parmesan Sticks

Delicious Garlic Butternut Squash

Lemon Rice with Toasted Pine Nuts

Spicy Corn Bread, Stuffed with Chilies and Cheese

Indian Corn Cakes

Risotto with Spinach and Gorgonzola Cheese

Crispy Corn Fritters

Sweet Potato and Black Bean Hash

Garlicky Parmesan Roasted Potatoes

Snow Peas with Ginger and Water Chestnuts

Cheesy Broccoli Rice

Kale, Squash, and Bean Medley

Garlic and Parmesan Mashed Potatoes

Balsamic Roasted Brussels Sprouts

Creamed Spinach

Brown Rice Pilaf with Toasted Almonds

Side Dishes

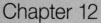

Chapter 12

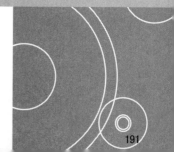

Simple Zucchini-Parmesan Sticks

Serves 4

1 cup zucchini, sliced into 2"–3"
  sticks
Nonstick cooking spray
Misto sprayer filled with extra-
  virgin olive oil
1 tablespoon shaved fresh
  Parmesan cheese
Salt and pepper, to taste

This is an easy, delicious side dish that complements any entrée. These are also perfect for a light, healthy snack.

1. Preheat the oven to broil. Line baking sheet with aluminum foil. Spray nonstick cooking spray on aluminum foil to prevent sticking.

2. Place sliced zucchini sticks on aluminum foil and spray lightly with olive oil sprayer.

3. Sprinkle Parmesan cheese on top. Season with salt and pepper.

4. Broil for a few minutes until cheese melts and turns light brown, about 2 minutes.

Delicious Garlic Butternut Squash

The name says it all! This is perfect, simple, and delicious. Butternut squash is low in calories and rich in vitamins and minerals. It's a wonderful alternative to potatoes.

1. Preheat the oven to 400°F.

2. In a large bowl, combine the parsley, oil, garlic, cheese, rosemary, salt, and pepper. Add the squash and toss to coat.

3. Transfer to an ungreased shallow 2-quart baking dish. Bake, uncovered, for 50–55 minutes or until squash is just tender.

Serves 6

2 tablespoons minced fresh parsley
1 tablespoon grapeseed oil
2 cloves garlic, minced
¼ cup freshly grated Parmesan cheese
½ teaspoon rosemary, dried
½ teaspoon kosher salt
½ teaspoon pepper
3½ pounds butternut squash, peeled and cut into 1" cubes

Butternut Squash

Butternut squash is a type of winter squash that is similar to pumpkin. Cutting up butternut squash can be a little intimidating. First, cut off ¼" from both ends. Use a sharp vegetable peeler and peel the outer layer of squash. Once completely peeled, slice squash in half from top to bottom. Next, scoop out the seeds and gummy pulp inside the squash. Cut each half into half, making quarters. Then chop each quarter into strips. Finally, slice each strip into cubes.

Lemon Rice with Toasted Pine Nuts

Serves 4

1 cup arborio rice
1½ cups water
1 tablespoon grapeseed oil
Juice from ½ lemon
1 clove garlic, finely chopped
Salt and pepper, to taste
Zest from 1 lemon
¼ cup fresh parsley
1 tablespoon pine nuts, toasted
1 tablespoon fresh Parmesan
    cheese (optional)

This dish can easily be made into a meal by simply adding chicken or sausage. The lemon flavor is so light and can easily go alongside most entrées.

1. In a large saucepan, combine the rice with water over high heat and bring to a boil. Reduce heat to medium, stirring continuously until the water is absorbed.

2. In ¼ cup increments, add an additional 3 cups of water to the saucepan. Continue to stir constantly while adding the water and until all 3 cups of water have been absorbed. Drain well, but do not rinse.

3. In a small bowl, mix the oil and lemon juice.

4. Transfer the rice to a medium-sized serving bowl. Add garlic, lemon juice mixture, and season with salt and pepper.

5. Add the lemon zest, parsley, and pine nuts, and toss. Top with Parmesan cheese if desired.

Arborio Rice

Arborio rice cooks much differently than other varieties of rice. Arborio rice is typically used in risotto dishes, which require a creamier texture. By slowly adding the water and continuously stirring, the rice releases starches, which make the texture much creamier.

Spicy Corn Bread, Stuffed with Chilies and Cheese

This is perfect with wheat-free soups, fried chicken, stews, and chowders. You can easily adjust the spices according to your taste.

1. Preheat the oven to 400°F. In a large bowl, mix together the cornmeal, flour, sugar, baking powder or baking soda, salt, cumin, and red pepper flakes.

2. Mix in the buttermilk, sour cream, eggs, and melted butter.

3. Prepare an 8" square baking pan with non-stick spray. Place half of the batter in the pan. Sprinkle with peppers and cheese. Cover with the rest of the batter. Bake for 20–25 minutes.

The Word on Chipotle

Chipotle chilies are jalapeño chili peppers that have been smoked and preserved in brine or vinegar. They are useful in cooking and baking, adding a smoky zing to recipes.

Serves 6–8

1 cup cornmeal (yellow or white)
1 cup corn or rice flour
¼ cup light brown sugar
3 teaspoons gluten-free baking powder or baking soda
1 teaspoon salt
¼ teaspoon cumin
1 teaspoon dried red pepper flakes, or to taste
½ cup buttermilk
½ cup sour cream, wheat-free
2 eggs, beaten
2 tablespoons unsalted butter, melted
½ cup chipotle chilies, chopped
½ cup grated pepper jack or Cheddar cheese

Indian Corn Cakes

Makes about 12 cakes

7 cups water
1 tablespoon salt, or to taste
2 cups cornmeal
½ teaspoon freshly ground
  black pepper, or to taste
1 teaspoon molasses
4 tablespoons butter or lard

This is delightful as a side dish or as an easy snack.

1. Bring the water to a boil and add salt. Stir in the cornmeal and cook for about 20 minutes, stirring occasionally. Add the pepper and molasses.

2. Prepare an 11" × 13" glass lasagna pan with nonstick spray. Spread the corn mixture in the pan and cover. Refrigerate for 1–2 hours, or until very stiff.

3. Heat butter or lard in a large frying pan. Cut the corn cakes into twelve squares and fry until golden on both sides about 3–4 minutes per side.

Corn Lore

Native Americans saved early settlers in this country with their stores of corn. Native Americans taught the colonists how to grow, dry, and mill corn into meal. Interestingly, corn, as a crop, started in ancient Mexico and Central America. The valuable crop went all the way to Canada, indicating tribal movement and sharing.

Risotto with Spinach and Gorgonzola Cheese

This is a wonderful complement to any poultry or seafood dish.

1. Bring the broth to a slow simmer in a saucepan and keep hot.

2. Heat the butter and oil in a large, heavy pan; add the onion and sauté until softened, about 8 minutes. Add the rice and stir. Add salt and pepper.

3. Add the broth, ¼ cup at a time, until it is all gone, stirring constantly. This will take about 35 minutes. If the rice is still not done, add water, ¼ cup at a time. When rice is cooked, add spinach, one handful at a time. Stir to combine.

4. Stir in the Gorgonzola cheese and garnish with strips of roasted red pepper and parsley. Serve hot.

Serves 4

5 cups canned or homemade chicken, fish, or vegetable broth, wheat-free

2 tablespoons butter

2 tablespoons extra-virgin olive oil

½ cup finely chopped sweet onion

1½ cups arborio rice, uncooked

Salt and freshly ground black pepper, to taste

10 ounces fresh spinach, rinsed and finely chopped

¼ cup crumbled Gorgonzola cheese

Roasted red pepper strips and chopped parsley, for garnish

Crispy Corn Fritters

Makes 12–14 fritters

1 egg
⅓ cup milk or wheat-free beer
⅔ cup cornstarch or corn flour
1½ teaspoons gluten-free baking powder
½ teaspoon salt
Red pepper flakes and/or ground black pepper, to taste
⅛ teaspoon freshly grated nutmeg
1 cup fresh corn, cut off the cob, or frozen
Peanut, canola, or other cooking oil (not olive oil)

Fritters are really fun to make and to eat. They can be as plain or as interesting as you want. The idea is to make them really creamy on the inside and crispy on the outside.

1. Starting with the egg and milk, place everything but the corn and oil in a food processor and blend until smooth. Scrape into a bowl; fold in the corn.

2. Heat about 1" of oil to 350°F in a large frying pan.

3. Drop the fritters by the tablespoonful into the hot oil and cook for 3–5 minutes. Drain on paper towels and serve hot.

Frittering Away

You can vary your fritters by using chopped clams instead of corn. They are fine with eggs for breakfast or as a side dish with chicken or steak. They are good with syrup or with wheat-free herb-savory gravy. You can also use them as hors d'oeuvres to dip in wheat-free salsa.

Sweet Potato and Black Bean Hash

This is a wonderful side dish and leftovers can easily be wrapped up in a wheat-free tortilla. Feel free to add chorizo or any kind of wheat-free sausage to make a complete meal.

1. Heat the olive oil over medium heat in a large skillet. Add onions and garlic and cook for 3–4 minutes.

2. Add the yellow pepper and cook another 2 minutes until they all start to brown.

3. Add the sweet potatoes and continue to stir while they brown. Cook for another 5 minutes. Add jalapeño pepper (if using), cumin, coriander, cayenne pepper, and chili powder. Stir to combine.

4. Add broth and continue to stir for 3–4 minutes, until liquid is absorbed.

5. Add beans and continue to stir, making sure everything is completely mixed. Add cilantro, and season with salt and pepper.

6. Can be served warm or cold. Garnish with sliced avocado, lime wedges, diced scallions, or wheat-free sour cream, if desired.

Serves 4

2 tablespoons extra-virgin olive oil
1 medium onion, thinly sliced
2 cloves garlic, minced
1 small yellow pepper, chopped
2 medium sweet potatoes, peeled and diced into ½" cubes
1 jalapeño pepper, seeded and minced (optional)
1½ teaspoons cumin
1 teaspoon coriander
⅛ teaspoon cayenne pepper, wheat-free
½ teaspoon chili powder, wheat-free
¾ cup vegetable broth, wheat-free
1 (15-ounce) can black beans, rinsed thoroughly and drained
2 tablespoons fresh cilantro, diced
Salt and pepper, to taste
Sliced avocado, lime wedges, diced scallions, or sour cream, for garnish (optional)

Garlicky Parmesan Roasted Potatoes

Serves 4

2 tablespoons extra-virgin olive oil

2 cloves garlic, minced

1 medium onion, finely chopped

1 teaspoon fresh basil, diced

1 teaspoon fresh rosemary, chopped

1 teaspoon fresh parsley, chopped

2 tablespoons fresh Parmesan cheese, grated

⅛ teaspoon crushed red pepper flakes

½ teaspoon salt

4 large red potatoes, scrubbed clean and sliced into cubes

This side dish is a perfect companion to any meat or poultry dish. These potatoes also make a wonderful accompaniment to eggs for breakfast or brunch. Using fresh herbs and Parmesan cheese is definitely better when roasting.

1. Preheat the oven to 450°F.

2. Place all the ingredients in a large resealable plastic bag. Close the bag and shake to evenly coat potatoes.

3. Spray a baking sheet with nonstick cooking spray. Spread potato mixture in an even layer on baking sheet. Place in oven for 40 minutes, making sure to stir potatoes occasionally.

4. Place oven on broil and cook potatoes 1–2 minutes, until they become browned and crispy. Remove from oven. Serve immediately.

Dried Herbs

If you would like to use dried herbs or don't have fresh herbs on hand, remember less is more. Dried herbs are usually stronger than fresh ones. Typically, you can cut the amount in half when using dried herbs.

Snow Peas with Ginger and Water Chestnuts

This is a lovely side dish that would go perfectly over a bed of rice. You can add tofu if you would like to add protein and keep it vegetarian. You can also add cooked beef or chicken.

1. Remove strings and ends of snow peas.

2. Melt butter over high heat in large skillet, add peas, water chestnuts, gingerroot, garlic, lemon juice, sesame seeds, and soy sauce.

3. Continue to cook over high heat, while stirring, until peas are crisp and tender. Serve immediately.

Serves 4

1 cup snow peas, washed
1 tablespoon butter, or 1 tablespoon sesame oil
½ cup water chestnuts, rinsed and drained
2 teaspoons fresh gingerroot, chopped
1 clove garlic, minced
Juice from ½ lemon
1 tablespoon sesame seeds
1 tablespoon wheat-free soy sauce

Cheesy Broccoli Rice

Serves 10

2 cups water

1 cup uncooked jasmine rice, rinsed

1 teaspoon, plus 2 tablespoons, butter

4 slices bacon, wheat-free

4 cups broccoli florets and stems, cleaned and trimmed, finely chopped

1 medium onion, chopped

2 cloves garlic, minced

½ cup mushrooms, diced

1 tablespoon cornmeal

1½ cups milk

2 cups shredded Gouda cheese (you can also use Cheddar, Swiss, or provolone), divided

You will find that many other broccoli rice casseroles use canned cream soups. Be careful cooking with those as they contain a lot of sodium and fat and some can contain wheat products.

1. Preheat the oven to 350°F.

2. In a large saucepan, place 2 cups of water and rice over high heat and bring to a boil. Cover, reduce heat to low and simmer about 10 minutes, until all the liquid has been absorbed and rice is tender. Remove from heat and fluff with fork. Cover again and let sit 5 minutes.

3. In a large skillet, melt 1 teaspoon butter over medium-high heat. Add bacon and cook until crisp while turning over several times. Remove bacon from skillet and place on paper towels to drain.

4. Place broccoli in a large saucepan. Add water to cover broccoli. Bring to boil over high heat and reduce heat to medium. Cook for 3–4 minutes, until broccoli is bright green and tender. Remove from heat, drain, and place broccoli in a 1½-quart casserole dish. Crumble bacon into small pieces.

5. In same skillet that you cooked bacon, add onion, garlic, and mushrooms. Cook for 2–3 minutes more, until mushrooms are softened.

6. Add cornmeal and mix to combine. Slowly add milk and continue stirring until sauce thickens about 4 minutes.

7. Add 1½ cups cheese and crumbled bacon. Stir.

8. Combine rice and cheese sauce with broccoli in casserole dish. Top with remaining ½ cup cheese. Bake for 20 minutes, or until cheese is completely melted and golden brown.

Kale, Squash, and Bean Medley

This makes a wonderfully well-balanced vegetarian meal. This can also be a lovely addition to a hearty steak or poultry dish.

1. In a large skillet, cook squash with vegetable broth, gingerroot, and rosemary over medium-low heat for about 8–10 minutes, until squash becomes tender.

2. Stir in butter, kale, cranberries, pecans, beans, and salt. Toss to coat. Serve immediately.

Serves 6–8

1 cup butternut squash, peeled and cut into 1" cubes (about ¾ pound)
¼ cup vegetable broth, wheat-free
1 teaspoon fresh gingerroot
1 teaspoon rosemary, dried
2 tablespoons butter
3 cups kale, trimmed and washed
¼ cup dried cranberries, wheat-free
¼ cup chopped pecans, toasted
½ cup white beans, rinsed and drained
1 teaspoon salt

Garlic and Parmesan Mashed Potatoes

Serves 6

4 cloves garlic, minced and divided
2½ pounds Yukon Gold potatoes, scrubbed clean, unpeeled and quartered
2 tablespoons butter, softened
½ cup buttermilk
2 tablespoons sour cream, wheat-free
½ teaspoon sage
1 teaspoon salt
¼ cup fresh Parmesan cheese, grated
Chopped green onion, for garnish

These mashed potatoes are so flavorful you don't need any gravy. This dish goes wonderfully with fish, steak, meat loaf, chicken, or turkey. The possibilities are endless.

1. Place 2 cloves of garlic and the potatoes in a large saucepan. Cover with water and bring to a boil over high heat. Once boiling, cover and reduce heat to low and simmer 20–25 minutes, until the potatoes are fork tender.

2. Drain the potatoes thoroughly and place back into saucepan.

3. In a small bowl, add butter, 2 remaining cloves minced garlic, buttermilk, sour cream, sage, and salt. Stir to combine.

4. Add cheese and stir well. Place garlic sauce over potatoes and mix well. Mash with potato masher or hand mixer on medium-high speed until desired consistency. Top with chopped green onions. Serve immediately.

Be Creative with Potatoes

Let your imagination go wild with potatoes! Gone are the days when you think of boring, lumpy, instant potatoes. Making your own mashed potatoes is easy. You can add whatever seasonings and additions you'd like.

Balsamic Roasted Brussels Sprouts

Even those who do not typically like Brussels sprouts will love these! This is a simple and tasty dish, delicious enough for a holiday dinner.

1. Preheat the oven to 400°F.

2. In a small bowl, mix together the oil, balsamic vinegar, garlic, and paprika.

3. Place Brussels sprouts and oil/vinegar mixture in a large resealable plastic bag. Make sure the bag is closed and shake to coat sprouts evenly. Season with salt and pepper.

4. Place sprouts on a baking sheet that is coated with nonstick cooking spray. Roast sprouts for 35 minutes, shaking pan every 5–8 minutes to make sure they are evenly browning.

5. Remove from oven when finished, season with some more salt. Serve immediately.

The Many Benefits of Brussels Sprouts

Brussels sprouts are part of the cabbage family and actually look like little cabbages. Brussels sprouts were first grown in Brussels, Belgium, hence the name. These sprouts are packed with vitamins C, A, and B.

Serves 6

3 tablespoons extra-virgin olive oil
2 tablespoons balsamic vinegar, wheat-free
1 clove garlic, minced
1 teaspoon sweet paprika, wheat-free
1½ pounds Brussels sprouts, bottoms trimmed, outer leaves removed, and halved
Salt and pepper, to taste

Creamed Spinach

Serves 10

3 (10-ounce) bags fresh spinach, chopped
¼ cup butter
3 cloves garlic, minced
½ teaspoon nutmeg
1 medium-sized shallot, minced
½ cup heavy cream
4 ounces Asiago cheese
½ cup fresh Parmesan cheese,
grated
Salt and pepper, to taste

This recipe is wonderful and can easily be doubled to feed a larger group. You can substitute half-and-half for the heavy cream to lighten this up.

1. Place spinach in a large stock pot, cover with water, and cook over medium-high heat until wilted, about 2–3 minutes. Remove from heat and drain in colander until most of the liquid is gone.

2. Place butter in large skillet and melt over medium heat. Add garlic, nutmeg, and shallot, and cook 3–4 minutes, until shallot is translucent.

3. Add spinach and slowly pour in heavy cream. Sprinkle in Asiago and Parmesan cheeses. Continue to stir until sauce thickens, about 4–5 minutes. Season with salt and pepper. Serve warm or hot.

Brown Rice Pilaf with Toasted Almonds

For best results, soak the brown rice overnight to help make it softer and lighter. This can be served as a side dish or paired with beans to create a perfect dish.

1. Place the almonds in small dry skillet over medium heat, stirring constantly for 3–4 minutes, until lightly browned. Place almonds in a small bowl.

2. In the small skillet, sauté the onion and garlic in oil. Cook until onion is translucent, about 5 minutes.

3. Add the rice and stir until thoroughly mixed, about 1 minute.

4. Add parsley, broth, and marjoram; cover and reduce heat to low.

5. Simmer until all the water is absorbed and the rice is fully cooked, about 45–50 minutes.

6. Uncover, fluff with fork and let stand for a few minutes. Stir in toasted almonds. Add salt and pepper, if desired.

Serves 6

⅓ cup almonds, slivered
1 tablespoon extra-virgin olive oil
1 large onion, finely chopped
3 cloves garlic, minced
1½ cups long grain brown rice
1 teaspoon dried parsley
3½ cups vegetable broth or low-sodium chicken broth, wheat-free
2 teaspoons dried marjoram, minced
Salt and pepper, to taste

Brown Rice with Baby Spinach, Tomatoes, and Grilled Turkey Sausage

Southern Fried Green Tomatoes

Stuffed Peppers with Veggie-Burger Filling and Spices

Beef-Flavored White Rice with Asian Spices

Spanish-Style Rice

Asian-Style Soup with Rice Noodles

Rice Flour Crepes

Stir-Fried Shrimp and Vegetables in Rice Crepe Wraps

Stuffed Artichokes with Lemon and Olives

Curried Lamb Grilled on Skewers

Coconut-Almond Ice Cream

Pumpkin-Spice Muffins

White Chicken Chili

Almond Butter–Raisin Cookies

Dairy- and Wheat-Free Dishes

Chapter 13

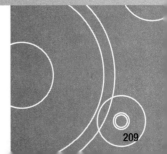

Brown Rice with Baby Spinach, Tomatoes, and Grilled Turkey Sausage

Serves 6

1½ cups brown rice, uncooked
1 (16-ounce) package turkey
    sausage, wheat-free
¼ teaspoon grapeseed oil
2 cloves garlic, chopped
2 cups organic baby spinach
½ pint grape or cherry tomatoes,
    sliced in half
1 yellow pepper, cut in 1" slices
¼ cup chicken broth, wheat-free
½ teaspoon sea salt
Pepper, to taste
½ teaspoon oregano
1 tablespoon fresh basil, torn

This dish will be a family favorite. It's so simple to make and can be made ahead of time.

1. Cook rice according to instructions.

2. Grill sausage in a grill pan or on the grill for 5–8 minutes, until browned and no longer pink. Set aside.

3. In a saucepan over medium heat, place oil and garlic, and sauté for 1–2 minutes, until garlic softens.

4. Add the spinach, tomatoes, and pepper and cook for 3–4 minutes, until vegetables are tender.

5. Add the chicken broth, salt, pepper, and oregano; turn heat to low and let simmer for 3–4 more minutes.

6. Add cooked sausage and stir to combine. Pour sausage/vegetable mixture over rice and serve immediately. Top with fresh basil.

Southern Fried Green Tomatoes

Use tomatoes that are very firm. They usually aren't very large, so count on two per person. Serve with thick slices of country ham or Irish bacon, wheat-free.

1. Combine corn flour with salt and pepper.

2. Spread the flour mixed with salt and pepper on one sheet of waxed paper and the cornmeal on another. Place the whisked eggs in a bowl between the two.

3. Dip the tomato slices first in the flour, then in the egg, and coat them with cornmeal.

4. Heat ½" of oil in a frying pan and heat to 350°F. Slide the tomato slices in and fry for 4 minutes or until well browned. Turn and finish frying, about 3–4 minutes.

5. Drain on paper towels. Serve as a side dish with eggs and bacon. This dish is perfect for brunch.

Serves 4

1 cup corn flour
Salt and coarsely ground black
    pepper, to taste
1 cup cornmeal
2 whole eggs whisked in a large
    flat soup bowl
8 green tomatoes, cores
    trimmed, cut in ⅓" slices
Oil for frying

Stuffed Peppers with Veggie-Burger Filling and Spices

Serves 4

4 large cloves garlic, minced
1 large onion, minced
¼ cup extra virgin olive oil
1 tablespoon Asian sesame oil
1 pound veggie burgers, wheat-free
Salt and pepper, to taste
4 large green or red bell peppers

Veggie burgers are typically well seasoned and quite delicious. They can be a great alternative to regular meats, although this recipe can also be prepared using ground beef, chicken, or turkey.

1. In a skillet over medium heat, sauté the garlic and onion in the olive and sesame oils until soft, about 3–4 minutes.

2. Add the veggie burgers, break them up into pieces with a wooden spoon, and stir. Add salt and pepper.

3. Preheat the oven to 350°F. Prepare a baking sheet with nonstick spray.

4. Cut the peppers in half lengthwise and scoop out seeds and cores. Fill with the burger mixture. Place on the baking sheet.

5. Bake for 25 minutes. Serve hot.

Dry Veggie Burgers?

You can do several things to keep veggie burgers moist. Adding a bit of chopped fresh tomato into the mix is one option. Another is to add olive oil before grilling. A bit of cooked, mashed potatoes (dairy-free if necessary) also adds bulk and moisture. Add about a tablespoon of tomato, oil, or mashed potato per burger.

Beef-Flavored White Rice with Asian Spices

This is the perfect side dish to complement any Asian-style stir-fry or grilled meat or fish. Five-spice powder is available at some supermarkets and at most Asian markets.

Mix together all ingredients except the rice to make a sauce. Boil to reduce for 3 minutes. Then mix in the rice, and serve hot.

A Grass, Not a Rice

Many people may be surprised to know that wild rice is not rice at all but a grass. Wild rice (*Zizania aquatica*) is really an annual aquatic seed found mostly in the upper freshwater lakes of North America. It was used by tribes such as the Algonquin and Ojibwa as an important food source and it was a staple in their ritual harvest feasts. Stores of wild rice nourished them during the long winters.

Serves 4

½ cup wheat-free soy sauce
¼ cup dry white wine or sake
1 tablespoon freshly grated gingerroot
1 tablespoon Asian sesame seed oil
1 teaspoon Asian five-spice powder, wheat-free
2 cloves garlic, minced
4 scallions, minced
⅔ cup beef broth, wheat-free
3 cups hot, cooked white rice

Spanish-Style Rice

Serves 4

3 cups water
2 teaspoons salt
1 cup white rice, uncooked
½ cup extra-virgin olive oil
1 large onion, chopped
1 clove garlic
½ teaspoon oregano, dried
2 jalapeño or poblano peppers,
    cored, seeded, and chopped
1 roasted red pepper, from a jar
    or your own, chopped
4 ripe plum tomatoes, cored and
    chopped
1 teaspoon lemon zest
10 black olives, sliced
Freshly ground black pepper,
    to taste

This is an excellent side to pair with a steak. Perfect for entertaining, it can be made in advance and then reheated just before serving time.

1. Bring the water to a boil, and add the salt and the rice. Reduce the heat to low, cover, and simmer until tender, about 25 minutes.

2. While the rice is cooking, heat the oil in a large frying pan.

3. Add the onion, garlic, oregano, and hot peppers. Sauté over low flame for 8–10 minutes.

4. Mix in the rest of the ingredients and simmer for 10 minutes.

5. Add to the hot rice and serve.

Ground Pepper

You can get pink, white, and black peppercorns. Some cooks like to mix them. Some say there is a taste difference among the three. Other cooks use white pepper in white food so you won't see the black specks. Try a coarsely ground pepper in recipes like the one above. To coarsely grind, place 6–8 peppercorns between two pieces of waxed paper. Use a heavy frying pan to press down on the corns until they are cracked and in coarse pieces. Don't just lay them on a board and hit them with the pan or they will fly all over the kitchen.

Asian-Style Soup with Rice Noodles

This can be served in small bowls as a first course or in large bowls as lunch. The contrast between soft and crunchy, spicy and sweet, makes this interesting and delicious.

1. Bring the chicken broth to a boil and add all but the tofu, noodles, and snow peas. Cover and simmer for 10 minutes. Add the tofu.

2. Stir gently and add the cooked noodles. Garnish with the snow peas and serve.

Serves 4

1 quart chicken broth, wheat-free
2 cloves garlic, minced
1"-piece fresh gingerroot, peeled and minced
1 bunch scallions, thinly sliced
12 canned water chestnuts
1 cup bean sprouts, well rinsed
½ cup dry sherry
½ cup wheat-free soy sauce
½ pound satin tofu
2 cups rice noodles, cooked
12 snow peas, sliced on the diagonal, for garnish

Rice Flour Crepes

Serves 4

2 eggs
1½ cups water or rice milk
½ teaspoon salt
¼ teaspoon freshly ground
   white pepper
1 cup rice flour
Peanut or canola oil

Use 1½ cups of rice milk instead of water if you want a richer crepe.

1. Place the eggs, water or rice milk, and salt in a blender and process them together. Add pepper and flour, stopping once to scrape the sides of the container.

2. Oil a nonstick pan, set heat to medium, and slowly pour or ladle small amounts (about ¼ cup) of the batter into the pan, lifting and tipping to spread the batter.

3. When the edges start to get brown, after about 3 minutes, flip the crepe. Cook for only 1 minute on the reverse side or it will become crisp and not pliable.

4. Cool and stack between sheets of waxed paper.

Crepes, Pancakes, and Tortillas— Ripe for the Stuffing

While gluten-free flours can be a disaster under certain circumstances, they are a great success when it comes to crepes, pancakes, and corn tortillas, which are made like crepes. You can stuff them like wontons, make tubes and fill them, or fold them and dip them into a spicy sauce. Experiment.

Stir-Fried Shrimp and Vegetables in Rice Crepe Wraps

These are wonderful as an appetizer or as an entrée. Feel free to dip them in teriyaki sauce (but read the label to make sure it is wheat free).

1. Heat the sesame and peanut oils in a wok or frying pan and add the vegetables and shrimp. Stir and cook until the shrimp turn pink, about 2–3 minutes.

2. Add the rest of the ingredients except for the crepes and the egg. Mix well. Place the shrimp and vegetables in a bowl and cool.

3. Put a spoonful of filling on half of a crepe. Paint the rim of the circle with the beaten egg. Fold over and press to seal.

4. Broil on high heat or steam the filled crepes for 10 minutes, or until they are steaming hot. Serve hot.

Serves 4

1 tablespoon sesame seed oil
¼ cup peanut oil
4 scallions, sliced
4 cloves garlic, minced
1 zucchini squash, finely chopped
1 medium onion, finely chopped
⅔ pound raw shrimp, shelled and deveined
½ cup almonds, chopped
1 tablespoon fish sauce, wheat-free
¼ cup dry sherry
1 teaspoon wasabi powder mixed with 2 teaspoons water to make a paste
1 recipe for Rice Flour Crepes (see recipe in this chapter)
1 egg, beaten

Stuffed Artichokes with Lemon and Olives

Serves 4 as an entrée, or 8 as an appetizer

4 large artichokes, trimmed and split lengthwise
4 quarts water
½ lemon
1 cup cooked rice
10 green olives, chopped
10 kalamata olives, chopped
2 tablespoons minced parsley
3 tablespoons grapeseed oil
1 teaspoon garlic salt
Pepper, to taste
1 egg (optional)

Artichokes have a way of making everything around them taste delicious. They can be eaten with just a little lemon juice.

1. Boil the artichokes in 4 quarts of water with squeezed lemon, and including rind, for 20 minutes. Drain and lay on a baking sheet, cut-side up.

2. Preheat the oven to 350°F.

3. Mix the rest of the ingredients (including the egg, if using) together in a large bowl.

4. Spoon the filling over the artichokes, pressing between the leaves. Bake for 15 minutes, until hot.

Curried Lamb Grilled on Skewers

Try grilling these and serving with your favorite wheat-free dipping sauce. They can be a huge crowd pleaser at a wedding reception or any occasion.

1. Soak 8–10 wooden skewers in water for at least 40 minutes.

2. Mix the peanut oil, curry, lemon juice, garlic, coriander, and hot sauce together in a bowl.

3. Add the lamb and turn to coat with the marinade. Cover and refrigerate for 2 hours.

4. String the lamb on the skewers and grill over hot coals for 4 minutes per side. Serve hot.

Serves 4

½ cup peanut oil
1 teaspoon curry powder, wheat-free
2 tablespoons lemon juice
4 cloves garlic, minced
½ teaspoon ground coriander
2 teaspoons wheat-free hot sauce, or to taste
1 pound bite-sized lamb chunks, from the leg or shoulder

Coconut-Almond Ice Cream

Serves 6

4 cups coconut milk (full fat)
½ cup honey
1 tablespoon wheat-free vanilla extract
½ cup toasted almonds, slivered

Even those who are not on a wheat- and dairy-free diet will love this ice cream! You can also add dairy-free carob chips or wheat-free chocolate chips to this ice cream.

1. Combine all the ingredients in a large mixing bowl. You might have to whisk to get the milk and honey to combine.

2. Prepare following your ice cream maker instructions. Store in the freezer for up to 2 weeks.

No Ice Cream Maker?

What happens if you don't have an ice cream maker? Don't fret. You can easily make this without one. Add all the ingredients except almonds in a blender or food processor and blend for 2–3 minutes, until thoroughly mixed. Make sure you stop to scrape the sides of the blender too. Take the mixture out of blender and pour into an airtight freezer safe container. Toss in almonds and stir to combine. Freeze for 6–8 hours, until it hardens.

Pumpkin-Spice Muffins

You will love these muffins, as they will leave you satisfied, and you will never miss the wheat or dairy.

1. Preheat the oven to 375°F. Spray muffin tins with baking spray or line with cupcake liners.

2. In a large bowl, mix all the ingredients together except for the ground flaxseed and the flour until thoroughly combined.

3. Add the ground flaxseed and flour slowly and mix to combine.

4. Bake for 35–40 minutes, until toothpick comes out clean when inserted in the middle of muffin.

Makes 18–24 muffins, depending on their size

1 (15-ounce) can puréed pumpkin
2 eggs
¼ cup canola oil
1 teaspoon wheat-free baking powder
½ cup turbinado sugar
½ cup 100% maple syrup
¼ teaspoon salt
1 tablespoon pumpkin pie spice
1 teaspoon ground cinnamon
½ teaspoon ground cloves
⅛ teaspoon ground ginger
1¼ cups flaxseed, ground
1 cup all-purpose, wheat-free flour

White Chicken Chili

Serves 6

1 tablespoon grapeseed oil
1 medium onion, chopped
4 cloves garlic, chopped
1 cup mushrooms, chopped
1½ cups frozen corn
½ cup chopped green bell
   pepper
1 (4-ounce) can chopped green
   chili peppers
1½ teaspoons ground cumin
¼ teaspoon ground cayenne
   pepper, wheat-free
½ teaspoon chili powder, wheat-
   free
1 teaspoon oregano
3 (15-ounce) cans navy white
   beans, rinsed and drained
2 (14.5-ounce) cans chicken
   broth, wheat-free
1½ pounds cooked skinless,
   boneless chicken breast,
   chopped
1 tablespoon cilantro, chopped
Chopped scallions or chopped
   cilantro, for garnish

This is the perfect comfort food any time of the year. Wheat-free corn bread would go perfectly with this dish.

1. Heat oil in a large pot or Dutch oven over medium-low heat, and add onion and garlic. Cook for 3–4 minutes, until onions become translucent.

2. Add mushrooms, corn, and bell pepper, and cook until they soften a bit, about 2–3 minutes.

3. Add chili peppers, cumin, cayenne pepper, chili powder, and oregano. Stir to combine.

4. Take 1 can of white beans and place in a blender or food processor until completely blended. You might need to add a bit of water if it becomes too thick.

5. Pour blended bean mixture into pot along with chicken broth, remaining 2 cans of beans, cooked chicken, and chopped cilantro, and stir. Reduce heat to low and continue to simmer about 10–15 minutes, stirring occasionally.

6. Top with chopped scallions or chopped cilantro.

Spice It Up

Do you like your chili a little spicier? Just add a fresh jalapeño (seeded and diced), or increase the cayenne pepper and chili powder. This dish can be made to suit your taste.

Almond Butter–Raisin Cookies

These cookies are so easy to make. You can use other nut butters if you'd like. They also freeze very well.

1. Preheat the oven to 350°F.

2. In a medium bowl, stir together all ingredients except raisins until blended.

3. Stir in raisins.

4. Drop dough by tablespoonfuls onto parchment-lined baking sheets. Bake for 10–15 minutes or until lightly browned.

5. Let cool on baking sheets for 5 minutes. Remove to a wire rack and let cool for 15 more minutes.

Makes 24 cookies

1 cup unsalted almond butter, stirred well

¾ cup coconut sugar or sugar of your choice

1 large egg

½ teaspoon baking soda

¼ teaspoon sea salt, omit if the almond butter is salted

1 teaspoon wheat-free vanilla extract

½ teaspoon cinnamon

3 ounces raisins (you can also use dried cranberries, apricots, dates, cherries, or dried fruit of your choice)

Double Chocolate-Quinoa Muffins

Quinoa "Mac and Cheese" in Tomato Bowls

Vegan Quinoa–Black Bean Cakes

Asiago Quinoa with Portobello Mushrooms

Quinoa Pilaf with Lentils and Spinach

Quinoa Meat Loaf

Quinoa Meatballs with Creamy Pesto Dipping Sauce

Pepperoni Pizza Quinoa Cups

Spicy Quinoa Bean Burgers

Spicy Black Quinoa, Sausage, and Goat Cheese

Mushroom and Squash Quinoa Risotto

Quinoa Pumpkin Chocolate Chip Squares

Quinoa Pudding with Fresh Raspberries

Quinoa

Chapter 14

Double Chocolate-Quinoa Muffins

Makes 12 muffins

1¾ cups buckwheat flour
¼ cup unsweetened cocoa
  powder
½ cup fine sugar
1½ teaspoons wheat-free baking powder
1 teaspoon sea salt
1 teaspoon cinnamon
¼ cup grapeseed oil
1 large egg
1 cup reduced fat buttermilk
1¼ teaspoons wheat-free vanilla
  extract
2 cups cooked quinoa, cooled
⅓ cup semi-sweet chocolate
  chips, wheat-free
¼ cup chopped almonds or
  whatever nuts you like

Quinoa adds a wonderful texture and a good amount of protein to these delicious chocolate muffins.

1. Preheat the oven to 350°F. Line muffin tins with cupcake liners or spray with baking spray.

2. Combine all the dry (the first 6) ingredients in a bowl and mix with a wire whisk.

3. In a separate, larger bowl, combine the wet ingredients (including the chocolate chips and nuts) and mix thoroughly.

4. Carefully fold in the dry ingredients and mix just until they are combined.

5. Fill muffin tins ¾ full with batter. Bake for 25 minutes, or until cooked through by inserting toothpick in the center and it comes out clean. Let cool slightly before removing from the pan.

Boost the Antioxidant Power

Why not add some ground flaxseed to increase your fiber and antioxidants? Simply add 2 tablespoons ground flaxseed to the second step and add omega-3 fatty acids, antioxidants, fiber, and protein.

Quinoa "Mac and Cheese" in Tomato Bowls

These yummy broiled tomatoes make delicious little bowls for this tasty quinoa dish.

1. Bring a pot of lightly salted water to a boil over high heat. Add the quinoa, and cook until the quinoa is tender, 15–20 minutes. Drain in a mesh strainer, and rinse until cold; set aside.

2. Heat the grapeseed oil in a skillet over medium heat, stir in pine nuts, and cook until lightly toasted, about 2 minutes.

3. Stir in the garlic, and cook until the garlic softens, about 2 minutes. Stir in the quinoa and spinach; cook and stir until the quinoa is hot, and the spinach has wilted, about 3–4 minutes. Stir in the lemon juice, and the cheese.

4. Meanwhile place tomatoes in a baking dish and place sliced top back on top of the tomato. Place in broiler for 5 minutes until they soften slightly but still remain intact.

5. Take tomatoes out and place the quinoa mixture inside the tomato, using them like bowls. The juices of the tomato will combine with the quinoa mixture and taste delicious.

Serves 4

¼ cup uncooked quinoa, rinsed and drained
1 tablespoon grapeseed oil
2 tablespoons pine nuts
2 cloves garlic, minced
1 cup fresh spinach leaves
Juice of ½ fresh lemon
¼ cup grated cheese of your choice
4 organic beefsteak tomatoes, top 1" sliced off, pulp and seeds scooped out

Quinoa's Superpowers

Quinoa has been popular lately because it is so versatile and can be used in so many different ways. Quinoa is actually a seed that is loaded with magnesium, iron, and calcium. Quinoa is just like a grain, but it is the only one to have all nine essential amino acids, which also makes it the only one to be a complete protein. It is low calorie, has a lot of fiber, and is also wheat and gluten free.

Vegan Quinoa–Black Bean Cakes

Makes 8 cakes

3 tablespoons grapeseed oil (or extra-virgin olive oil)

½ cup finely chopped green bell pepper

3 cloves garlic, chopped

1 medium onion, finely chopped

½ cup finely chopped plum tomatoes

1 (15-ounce) can organic black beans, thoroughly rinsed and drained

2 cups quinoa, cooked in wheat-free vegetable broth

1 tablespoon fresh cilantro leaves

½ teaspoon cumin

½ teaspoon red pepper flakes

Salt and pepper, to taste

1 egg white, beaten

1 cup wheat-free bread crumbs

Fresh cilantro and diced tomatoes, for garnish (optional)

These are so light and tasty that they can be made with a green salad for an entrée or even served as an appetizer.

1. Heat 2 tablespoons of grapeseed oil in skillet; add the green pepper and sauté until soft, about 3 minutes.

2. Add the garlic, onion, and tomatoes, and continue to sauté until soft, about 3–4 minutes.

3. Remove from heat, combine with black beans, quinoa, cilantro, cumin, and red pepper flakes. Allow to cool for a few minutes. Add salt and pepper to taste. Place in food processor and pulse until chunky but not completely smooth.

4. Add the beaten egg white and mix well. Form into patties, dredge in bread crumbs, and place in heated skillet with 1 tablespoon grapeseed oil. Sauté at least 5 minutes on each side. Garnish with fresh cilantro and diced tomatoes.

Asiago Quinoa with Portobello Mushrooms

This dish can be kept vegetarian, or you can also include diced shrimp or chicken to add some protein. In addition, you can throw in whatever fresh vegetables you have on hand to add some color.

1. Heat 1 tablespoon of oil in a large skillet. Add the shallot, garlic, and mushrooms. Top with the thyme and oregano and cook until browned, about 5 minutes. Set aside.

2. Heat the other tablespoon of oil in a pot over medium-high heat. Add quinoa and let it brown, about 2–3 minutes. Pour in the vegetable broth and bring it to a boil. Cover and reduce heat to low. Simmer for 15–20 minutes, until all the liquid is absorbed.

3. Stir in mushroom mixture and top with basil and cheese.

Are Shallots the Same as Green Onions?

No, they are not. Shallots are often confused for green onions or scallions. They are, however, members of the onion family, with their own mild taste. Shallots look like small onions, which when peeled, have divided cloves like garlic. When a recipe calls for 1 shallot, they generally mean the entire shallot, not just one clove.

Serves 6

2 tablespoons extra-virgin olive oil
1 shallot, chopped
2 cloves garlic, minced
1 cup portobello mushrooms, wiped clean, stems removed and sliced
1 teaspoon thyme
1 teaspoon oregano
1½ cups uncooked quinoa, rinsed and drained
2½ cups vegetable broth, wheat-free
2 tablespoons fresh basil, torn
⅓ cup Asiago cheese, grated

Quinoa Pilaf with Lentils and Spinach

Serves 4

1 tablespoon butter
½ medium onion, finely chopped
1 clove garlic, minced
½ cup uncooked quinoa, rinsed and drained
1½ cups vegetable broth, wheat-free
½ cup uncooked lentils, rinsed and dried
1 tablespoon extra-virgin olive oil
1 cup water
2 carrots, finely chopped
1 teaspoon oregano, dried
1 teaspoon basil, dried
4 cups baby spinach
Salt and pepper, to taste
¼ cup toasted almonds, for garnish (optional)

This dish is loaded with protein; it makes the perfect vegetarian dish.

1. Place butter in large skillet over medium heat. Add onion and garlic and cook 3–4 minutes, until onion is translucent.

2. Add rinsed quinoa and let sit for 1 minute until brown. Add broth and bring to a boil. Reduce heat, cover, and let simmer on low heat until all broth is absorbed, about 15–20 minutes.

3. While quinoa is cooking, place dried lentils and olive oil in a small skillet. Add water, carrots, oregano, and basil. Bring water to slight boil over medium-high heat, then reduce heat to low. Cook lentils for 20–30 minutes, until tender.

4. When quinoa is finished cooking, stir in baby spinach. Add salt and pepper.

5. Combine lentil mixture and quinoa together. Garnish with toasted almonds if desired.

Watch the Dates on Your Lentils

Try not to mix older lentils with fresh ones. Older lentils may take longer to cook than the newer ones because they have lost moisture. This will leave the fresh lentils overcooked and mushy.

Quinoa Meat Loaf

You won't miss the bread crumbs in this recipe. Quinoa adds protein and texture to your typical meat loaf.

1. Bring the quinoa and broth to a boil in a saucepan over high heat. Reduce heat to medium-low, cover, and simmer until the quinoa is tender and the water has been absorbed, about 15–20 minutes. Set aside to cool.

2. Preheat the oven to 350°F.

3. Heat the olive oil in a skillet over medium heat. Add in the onion; cook and stir until the onion has softened and turned translucent, about 5 minutes. Add the garlic and cook for another minute; remove from heat to cool.

4. In a large bowl add the chicken, cooked quinoa, onions, garlic, tomato paste, Worcestershire sauce, egg and egg white, salt, pepper, seasonings, and Parmesan cheese. Mix until well combined. The mixture will be very moist. Shape into a loaf on a foil-lined baking sheet.

5. Bake until no longer pink in the center, 50–60 minutes. An instant-read thermometer inserted into the center should read at least 160°F. Let the meat loaf cool for 10 minutes before slicing and serving.

Serves 6

¼ cup uncooked quinoa, rinsed and drained

½ cup chicken broth, wheat-free

1 teaspoon extra-virgin olive oil

1 small onion, chopped

2–3 cloves garlic, chopped

1 (20-ounce) package lean ground chicken (or lean ground turkey or beef)

1 tablespoon tomato paste

2 teaspoons wheat-free Worcestershire sauce

1 egg, and 1 egg white

½ teaspoons salt

1 teaspoon ground black pepper

1 teaspoon ground rosemary

1 teaspoon ground basil

¾ teaspoon red pepper flakes

2 tablespoons fresh Parmesan cheese, grated

Quinoa Meatballs with Creamy Pesto Dipping Sauce

Serves 6

¼ cup uncooked quinoa, rinsed and drained

½ cup chicken broth, wheat-free

1 teaspoon extra-virgin olive oil

1 small onion, chopped

2–3 cloves garlic, chopped

1 (20-ounce) package lean ground chicken (or lean ground turkey or beef)

1 tablespoon tomato paste

2 teaspoons wheat-free Worcestershire sauce

1 egg, and 1 egg white

1 teaspoon ground rosemary

1 teaspoon ground basil

¾ teaspoon red pepper flakes

2 tablespoons fresh Parmesan cheese, grated

½ teaspoons salt

1 teaspoon ground black pepper

Creamy Pesto Dipping Sauce (see Chapter 11)

These meatballs make the perfect appetizer or main dish. Serve with zucchini noodles or wheat-free pasta.

1. Preheat the oven to 350°F.

2. Bring the quinoa and broth to a boil in a saucepan over high heat. Reduce heat to medium-low, cover, and simmer until the quinoa is tender and the water has been absorbed, about 15–20 minutes. Set aside to cool.

3. Heat the olive oil in a skillet over medium heat. Stir in the onion; cook and stir until the onion has softened and turned translucent, about 5 minutes. Add the garlic and cook for another minute; remove from heat to cool.

4. In a large bowl, combine the chicken, cooked quinoa, onions, garlic, tomato paste, Worcestershire sauce, egg and egg white, seasonings, Parmesan cheese, salt, and pepper. Mix until well combined. The mixture will be very moist.

5. Roll into 1½" balls. Place onto a baking sheet lined with parchment paper.

6. Bake until no longer pink in the center, 20–25 minutes. Serve with pesto dipping sauce.

Pepperoni Pizza Quinoa Cups

These make fun appetizers or a great entrée. The whole family will love them. They also freeze really well, so feel free to double this recipe and store half in the freezer.

1. Preheat the oven to 350°F. Spray a muffin tray with nonstick cooking spray.

2. Place all the ingredients in a medium-sized mixing bowl. Stir thoroughly to combine.

3. Pour the quinoa mixture into muffin tins. Bake for 15–20 minutes, until cheese is melted.

4. Let stand for 5–10 minutes to cool before serving. Serve with Easy Pizza Sauce for dipping.

Makes 12 quinoa cups

1 cup cooked quinoa
3 cloves garlic, minced
½ cup pepperoni, diced (be sure it is wheat-free)
1 medium onion, finely chopped
1 cup shredded mozzarella cheese
¼ cup finely minced mushrooms
1 teaspoon oregano, dried
1 teaspoon basil, dried
½ teaspoon wheat-free paprika, dried
½ teaspoon rosemary, dried
½ teaspoon fennel seed
2 large eggs
½ cup grape tomatoes, diced
1 teaspoon tomato paste
Easy Pizza Sauce, for dipping (see Chapter 15)

Spicy Quinoa Bean Burgers

Makes 6 burgers

½ cup uncooked quinoa, rinsed and drained
1 cup vegetable broth, wheat-free
1 (15-ounce) can black beans, rinsed and drained
1 (15-ounce) can red kidney beans, rinsed and drained
1 cup baby spinach
¾ cup cornmeal or wheat-free bread crumbs
¼ cup red bell pepper, chopped
¼ cup frozen corn, defrosted
¼ cup mushrooms, finely diced
1 shallot, minced
1 clove garlic, minced
1 teaspoon chili powder, wheat-free
½ teaspoon red pepper flakes
1 teaspoon cumin
1 teaspoon paprika, wheat-free
1 teaspoon fresh cilantro, chopped
1 teaspoon wheat-free hot sauce
1 egg
Juice of ½ fresh lime
Fresh avocado slices and tomato slices for topping

Even meat lovers will love these burgers! The patties can be made ahead of time and then refrigerated until ready to cook.

1. Preheat the oven to 375°F.

2. Place the quinoa and broth in a small saucepan and bring to a boil. Cover, reduce heat to low, and simmer for 15–20 minutes, until all the broth is absorbed.

3. Place the beans and spinach in blender or food processor and process for 1 minute, allowing for some pieces of whole beans to remain.

4. Place the quinoa in a medium-sized bowl. Add the beans/spinach mixture, cornmeal, bell pepper, corn, mushrooms, shallot, garlic, seasonings, cilantro, hot sauce, egg, and fresh lime juice. Thoroughly mix with your hands to combine. If you have time, sit bowl in the refrigerator for a few minutes. This allows for easier forming of the patties.

5. Form the quinoa/bean mixture into 6 patties. Line baking sheet with aluminum foil and place patties on top. Bake for 30 minutes, making sure to turn them over after first 15 minutes.

6. Serve on top of rice or sautéed spinach and top with avocado and tomato slices. You can also eat these burgers with a wheat-free bun, in a wheat-free wrap or wrap each one in a giant lettuce leaf.

No Wheat-Free Bread Crumbs in the House?

Ground rolled oats are a wonderful substitute for wheat-free bread crumbs. Just make sure you read your labels to guarantee your rolled oats are wheat-free!

Spicy Black Quinoa, Sausage, and Goat Cheese

This recipe may be called spicy, but you can always adjust the spices and seasonings according to your taste. You can also use sweet sausage if chorizo is too spicy. Black quinoa makes a lovely presentation too.

1. Place the chicken broth into a medium saucepan and bring to a boil over high heat. Add quinoa and cover. Reduce heat and let simmer 15–20 minutes, until all liquid is absorbed. Remove from heat. Fluff with a fork and place into a large bowl.

2. While the quinoa cooks, place the oil in a large skillet along with onion and garlic. Cook over medium heat for 3–4 minutes, until they soften.

3. Add the chorizo and cook until browned and no longer pink inside, about 8–10 minutes. Remove from the skillet and cut into ½"-thick rounds. Place chorizo in the bowl with the quinoa.

4. In the same skillet, add the peppers, tomatoes, cumin, and red pepper flakes. Stir well and cook over medium heat for about 5 minutes, until vegetables soften.

5. Add the cooked vegetables to the bowl with the quinoa and chorizo. Top with goat cheese and stir to combine. Add salt and pepper to taste if desired.

Serves 4

2 cups chicken broth, wheat-free

1 cup black quinoa, uncooked, rinsed, and drained

1 tablespoon extra-virgin olive oil

½ green onion, diced

2 cloves garlic, minced

2 links Mexican chorizo, wheat-free

1 red or yellow pepper, seeded and chopped

1 green pepper, seeded and chopped

½ cup grape or cherry tomatoes, halved

¼ teaspoon cumin

⅛ teaspoon red pepper flakes

¼ cup goat cheese

Salt and pepper, to taste

Mushroom and Squash Quinoa Risotto

Serves 4–6

1 cup quinoa, rinsed
1½ cups vegetable broth, wheat-free (can also use wheat-free chicken broth)
1 tablespoon butter
2 cloves garlic, minced
½ onion, minced
2 cups diced butternut squash
2 cups sliced mushrooms
1 tablespoon dried oregano
½ teaspoon dried marjoram
½ teaspoon dried sage
½ teaspoon cinnamon
½ cup dry white wine
¼ cup freshly grated Parmesan cheese

This dish has a unique twist on traditional risotto made with rice. This can be left vegetarian or would also taste wonderful with sliced sweet sausage added to it.

1. Place quinoa and broth into a pot. Bring to a boil over medium heat. Cover and reduce heat to low. Simmer for 15–20 minutes until all liquid is absorbed.

2. While quinoa is cooking, place the butter, garlic, and onion into large skillet. Cook over medium heat 3–4 minutes until onions are translucent.

3. Add squash and let cook for 10 minutes or until squash softens.

4. Add mushrooms and seasonings, stir to combine.

5. Pour in the white wine and mix. Let cook for a few minutes until all the wine is absorbed. Add cooked quinoa to skillet and thoroughly combine.

6. Top with grated cheese and serve immediately.

Quinoa Pumpkin Chocolate Chip Squares

Quinoa adds a wonderful texture, protein, antioxidants, and fiber to these squares. You won't feel guilty having a second!

1. Preheat the oven to 350°F. Spray a 9" × 9" or 9" × 13" baking dish with nonstick cooking spray.

2. Mix flour, flax, pumpkin pie spice, cinnamon, baking soda, and salt in a medium-sized bowl. Set the bowl aside.

3. In a large bowl, mix the sugar, syrup, and butter until thoroughly combined. Add egg, quinoa, and vanilla and mix again.

4. Slowly add in pumpkin and continue to mix well. Once completely mixed, slowly add flour mixture. Feel free to add small amounts of water in increments of 1 teaspoon if batter seems too thick.

5. Once the flour mixture is thoroughly mixed, add chocolate chips and mix well.

6. Place in oven and bake for 40 minutes or until you place a toothpick in the center and it comes out clean. Allow to cook for 15 minutes before cutting into squares.

Makes 20 squares

2 cups wheat-free all purpose flour
½ cup ground flaxseed
1 teaspoon pumpkin pie spice, wheat-free
1½ teaspoons cinnamon
1 teaspoon baking soda
½ teaspoon salt
2 tablespoons turbinado sugar
3 tablespoons 100% pure maple syrup
½ cup butter, room temperature
1 egg
1 cup cooked quinoa, cooled
1½ teaspoons wheat-free vanilla extract
1½ cups pumpkin puree
¾ cup dark chocolate chips, wheat-free

Quinoa Pudding with Fresh Raspberries

Serves 4–6

2 cups uncooked quinoa
2 cups reduced fat milk (the more fat in the milk, the creamier the consistency)
½ cup half-and-half
3 tablespoons sugar
2 tablespoons maple syrup
1 teaspoon cinnamon
2 teaspoons wheat-free vanilla extract
½ teaspoon cinnamon
Fresh raspberries, to top pudding

Who said you can't make pudding a little healthier? This tastes similar to tapioca pudding, with a slightly nutty taste and thicker texture.

1. Place the quinoa in a fine mesh sieve and rinse under cold water for 1 minute.

2. In a large saucepan, whisk together the milk, half-and-half, sugar, maple syrup, 1 teaspoon cinnamon, and vanilla extract. Bring to a simmer over medium heat. Cook for 25 minutes, stirring occasionally, until creamy.

3. Add quinoa and ½ teaspoon of cinnamon. Turn heat down to low and allow to simmer for 20 minutes, or until desired consistency is reached. Stir every few minutes to prevent a film from forming on top of the pudding or on bottom of the pan.

4. Serve chilled, topped with raspberries (or fruit of your choice).

Why Do You Have to Rinse Quinoa Before Cooking?

Rinsing quinoa is important because of its outer coating, called saponin. Saponin has a bitter taste and can be unpleasant after it's cooked. You can also soak the quinoa if you'd like, but usually rinsing it for a minute or two does the trick.

Kid Friendly

Chapter 15

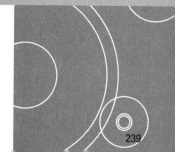

Parmesan-Flax-Crusted Chicken Tenders

Serves 4

2 egg whites and 1 whole egg, beaten
1 cup ground flaxseed
1 teaspoon dried basil
1 teaspoon dried oregano
1½ teaspoons red pepper flakes
2 cloves garlic, minced
½ teaspoon salt
½ teaspoon ground black pepper
⅓ cup Parmesan cheese, freshly grated
1 (16-ounce) package organic chicken tenderloins

These tenders are so tasty, the whole family will love them. Kids love to dip, so experiment with different wheat-free dipping sauces too.

1. Preheat the oven to 350°F. Spray 9" × 13" casserole dish with cooking spray.

2. Place egg whites and egg in a large bowl.

3. In a separate large bowl, place ground flax-seed, basil, oregano, red pepper flakes, garlic, salt, pepper, and cheese. Stir until mixed.

4. Start by placing each chicken tender in egg mixture, then coat with flax mixture, and make sure it is thoroughly coated on both sides. Place in prepared casserole dish.

5. Place casserole dish in the oven and cook for 35 minutes, making sure to turn tenders over halfway through cooking time. Serve with your favorite dipping sauce!

Homemade Is Better

Chicken tenders you find in the grocery store can have a lot of preservatives and ingredients in them that you may not expect. This recipe is a perfect example of how easy they are to make at home.

Grilled Cheese

This recipe is one of the hundreds of goodies you can make with No Grain Bread (see Chapter 2). Feel free to add some sliced tomatoes in there too for a kick of nutrition!

1. Arrange bread squares on a baking sheet that you have prepared with nonstick spray. Preheat the oven to 350°F.

2. Process the rest of the ingredients in the food processor until mixed. Don't worry about making the cheese mixture smooth. Using a teaspoon, place a small mound of cheese/ butter mixture on each bread square.

3. Bake until the cheese melts, about 10 minutes. You can vary this recipe by adding different herbs, chopped garlic, or any of your favorite flavors.

Stuffing and Spreads

Making spreads and stuffing for any number of things is a great way to use leftovers. You can take a chunk of leftover Brie cheese and put it in the food processor with some chopped onion and a bit of butter or margarine and have a whole new experience. Leftover chicken is excellent for making many different spreads, filling for stuffed celery, or a little sandwich.

Makes 32 small squares

1 loaf No Grain Bread (see Chapter 2), cut into squares
½ cup soft butter
1 cup cubed Monterey jack cheese
½ cup freshly grated Parmesan cheese
½ cup red roasted peppers (jarred is fine)
½ cup chopped sweet red onion

Popcorn with Parmesan Topping

Serves 8

1 tablespoon grapeseed oil
1 cup popcorn kernels
½ teaspoon sea salt
½ cup Parmesan cheese,
    freshly grated

There is no need to add butter to this popcorn. Parmesan cheese adds a delightful flavor to your typical, ordinary popcorn.

1. Place grapeseed oil in bottom of a large pot.

2. Place popcorn kernels on top of the oil in the pan. Do NOT turn stove on yet. Stir kernels to make sure they are evenly coated with the oil.

3. Place heat on medium and, and with the pot uncovered, shake the kernels around in the pot until the first kernel pops. Quickly place the lid on top and wait until all the kernels pop.

4. Once done, remove from heat and add salt and Parmesan cheese. Stir to mix thoroughly. You can store popcorn in an airtight container for up to 6 months.

Get Creative with Your Popcorn!

There are so many different seasonings you can add to your popcorn that won't add calories, fat, or additives. Wheat-free chili powder, curry, garlic powder, lemon pepper, or even sugar and cinnamon are among the many options you have. This is a perfect opportunity for children to experiment with new flavors too.

Baby Back Ribs

You can use any kind of wheat-free barbecue sauce you wish for this recipe. The trick is to cook the ribs in the sauce.

1. Fry the ribs in vegetable oil, turning, over medium-high heat until lightly brown, about 3–4 minutes each side.

2. Add the rest of the ingredients and cover. Cook over very low heat for 1 hour.

3. Remove the ribs and continue cooking the sauce until it is reduced to 1 cup, about 5–8 minutes. Serve sauce with ribs for dipping.

Serves 4–6

4 pounds baby back ribs, cut
  into 1-rib servings
½ cup vegetable oil
1 cup Easy Barbecue Sauce
  (see recipe in this chapter)
1 teaspoon garlic powder
1 cup tomato juice
½ cup orange juice

Easy Barbecue Sauce

Makes 8 servings (1 cup)

1 tablespoon cider vinegar, wheat-free

½ cup ketchup

1 tablespoon honey

2 tablespoons brown sugar

1 teaspoon garlic powder

½ tablespoon onion powder

1 tablespoon red pepper flakes

1 teaspoon wheat-free Dijon mustard

2 tablespoons wheat-free Worcestershire sauce

¼ teaspoon salt

You will never want to use store-bought barbecue sauce again after you make this. This zesty sauce is perfect for chicken, pork, or beef. You can keep this in an airtight container in the refrigerator for a few weeks.

1. Place all the ingredients in a small saucepan over medium heat.

2. Bring to a boil, turn heat to low, and simmer on low for a few minutes, stirring.

3. Allow to cool before brushing onto meat.

Chili Bean Dip with Dipping Vegetables

This is the perfect after-school snack for hungry children. Feel free to eliminate the jalapeño if it's too spicy for the little ones.

1. Sauté the beef in the oil with the onion, peppers, and garlic in a large skillet, breaking up any clumps with a spoon.

2. When the vegetables are soft, add the rest of the ingredients (except the cheese and vegetables for dipping). Cover and simmer for 1 hour.

3. Serve warm. Top with shredded cheese if desired. Or cool, and turn this into a dip by pulsing it in the food processor. Do not make it smooth. Serve alongside veggies.

Chili and Beans

There are endless variations of the chili-and-bean combination. Some people use turkey, others add dark chocolate and cinnamon and vary the amounts of beans and tomatoes. Some forms of chili don't have any beans. Different regions use various amounts of spice, heat, and ingredients.

Makes 1 quart

½ pound lean ground beef
1 tablespoon extra-virgin olive oil
1 medium onion, chopped
2 jalapeño peppers, or to taste, cored, seeded, and chopped
2 cloves garlic, chopped
¼ teaspoon ground pepper
4 teaspoons wheat-free chili powder, or to taste
1 (13-ounce) can crushed tomatoes with juice
1 (13-ounce) can red kidney beans
½ cup flat wheat-free beer
Cheddar cheese, shredded for topping (optional)
Assortment of carrots, celery pieces, radishes, broccoli, spears of zucchini, etc.

Grilled Chicken Wings

Serves 4–8

4 pounds chicken wings, split at
   the joint, tips removed
1 tablespoon onion powder
1 tablespoon garlic powder
¼ teaspoon cinnamon
2 teaspoons dark brown sugar
½ teaspoon paprika, wheat-free
½ teaspoon ground black
   pepper
¼ cup freshly squeezed lime
   juice
¼ cup extra-virgin olive oil
1 teaspoon salt
Ground black pepper, to taste

Traditional Buffalo wings are generally fried. This recipe, done with a rub and some olive oil, is a lot less fattening. Double the recipe and refrigerate half for delicious cold snacks.

1. Rinse the wings, and set them on paper towels to dry.

2. In a large bowl, mix the rest of the ingredients together. Coat the chicken with the spice mixture, cover, and refrigerate for 1 hour.

3. Grill over medium-hot coals or broil at 350°F for 20 minutes, turning every few minutes, or until well browned.

Spaghetti Squash with Marinara Sauce

Spaghetti squash holds endless possibilities for a nutritious, wheat-free diet. It's delicious and so easy to prepare.

1. Preheat the oven to 275°F.

2. Make a boat of aluminum foil and place the squash in the center and place on a baking sheet. Pierce the squash in several places with a knife to let the steam escape. Sprinkle with water. Tent with more foil and roast for 2 hours. The squash is done when you can insert a fork easily.

3. Cool the squash so you can handle it. Cut it in half and scoop out the seeds. Using a fork, run it through the flesh and it will turn into "spaghetti."

4. Mix the squash and most of the cheese together in a medium bowl and reheat. Sprinkle with the remaining cheese, garlic, and herbs then toss with marinara and serve.

Freshly Grated Cheese

Blocks of Parmesan cheese will keep for a week, tightly wrapped, in the refrigerator. It is so easy to grate exactly the amount you need, when you need it, and it tastes 100 percent better than the grated cheese you get in a box or jar. Use a box grater and place a piece of waxed paper on a cutting board. Grate away, then remove the grater, make a funnel of the paper, and slide the cheese into a bowl or add it to what you are preparing. You can also use Romano, fontina, or Cheddar cheese in this way and enjoy them so much more.

Serves 6–8

1 (4-pound) spaghetti squash, rinsed
1 cup freshly grated Parmesan cheese
1 clove garlic, minced
Garnish of fresh herbs such as parsley, basil, and oregano
2 cups of your favorite jarred, wheat-free marinara sauce

Tropical Fruit Salsa

Makes about 1½ cups

1 large mango, peeled, seeded, and diced
1 cup fresh pineapple, diced
½ red bell pepper, seeded and diced
¼ cup minced red onion
½ teaspoon freshly grated lime zest
Juice of ½ lime
Salt, to taste

The sweet blend of fruits and vegetables make a wonderful and unique salsa. Try it with pork, lamb, or any kind of fish. It is also great eaten with Brown Rice Chips (see Chapter 16).

Mix all ingredients in a bowl and cover. Refrigerate for 2 hours. Serve at room temperature.

Does Slicing Onions Make You Cry?

Place peeled and unsliced onions in a bowl of water for a few minutes before slicing. This little water soaking helps reduce some of the onion's harsh acids, which can cause tearing.

Banana-Nutter Sandwich

Move over PB & J, there's a new sandwich in town. This one is wheat-free and uses bananas instead of jelly.

1. Slice loaf of bread into 12 slices.

2. Spread peanut butter on 6 slices, then add sliced bananas. Place remaining bread slices on top to make a sandwich.

Wrap It Up!

These sandwiches are just as delicious when you use wheat-free wraps. Simply spread peanut butter on a wrap, top with banana slices and roll it up! Feel free to substitute other nut butters as well.

Serves 6

1 loaf No Grain Bread (see Chapter 2)
½ cup natural peanut butter
3–4 large bananas, sliced

Pepperoni Pizza Quesadillas

Serves 4

8 corn or brown rice flour
    tortillas, wheat-free
2 cups Easy Pizza Sauce (see
    recipe in this chapter), plus
    extra for dipping
8 ounces shredded mozzarella
    cheese
⅓ pound pepperoni
Sliced mushrooms, peppers,
    onions (optional)

What happens when pizza meets a wheat-free tortilla? You get Pizza Quesadillas that your whole family will love.

1. Brush each tortilla with a thin layer of pizza sauce (so thin that if you turned it over, none would drip).

2. Sprinkle cheese on top of the sauce on the bottom tortilla. Top with pepperoni and other toppings, if desired. Sprinkle with another layer of cheese and place the other tortilla on top (sauce side in).

3. Lay out tortilla and place it on a griddle or in a pan sprayed with cooking spray and cook for 3–5 minutes on each side, until cheese is melted and tortillas are crispy.

4. Slice into quarters and serve with a little bowl of pizza dipping sauce.

Easy Pizza Sauce

This delicious sauce will enhance the flavor of any type of pizza you make. This also makes a wonderful dipping sauce for quesadillas, chicken tenders, or even French fries.

1. In a skillet over medium heat, place the oil, garlic, and onions. Simmer until they soften, about 2–3 minutes.

2. In a medium bowl, mix together tomato sauce and tomato paste until smooth. Stir in oregano, basil, sugar, and salt. Add the cooked garlic and onions. Makes sauce for about 4 (10") pizzas.

Makes 2¾ cups

1 teaspoon extra-virgin olive oil
1–2 cloves garlic, finely chopped
½ medium onion, finely chopped
1 (15-ounce) can tomato sauce
1 (6-ounce) can tomato paste
1 tablespoon ground oregano
1 teaspoon ground basil
½ teaspoon turbinado sugar
½ teaspoon salt

Fruit Kebabs with Yogurt Dipping Sauce

Makes 4–6 kebabs

1 (16-ounce) container strawberries, sliced
1 kiwi, sliced
¼ cantaloupe, scooped out with
 melon baller
1 apple, cut into squares
¼ honeydew, scooped out with
 melon baller
Juice of ½ a lemon
Yogurt Dipping Sauce (see
 recipe in this chapter)

This is a really fun way to get the little ones to eat fruit. Be sure to cut the ends off the skewers for safety.

1. Place sliced fruit in any order on skewers with ends cut off.

2. Sprinkle with fresh lemon juice to ensure the fruit stays fresh.

3. Serve with Yogurt Dipping Sauce, or even melted chocolate or nut butter.

It's a Marshmallow World
Why not add some mini marshmallows to these fun kebabs? Marshmallows turn this delicious snack into a wonderful dessert. Check labels to ensure they are wheat-free!

Yogurt Dipping Sauce

The thickness of Greek yogurt and the sweetness of the honey make this a perfect dip for any fruit out there.

Mix all the ingredients in a small bowl. Serve immediately or store, covered, in the refrigerator.

Why Greek Yogurt?
Greek yogurt adds significantly more protein than regular yogurt. The thick texture of Greek yogurt is perfect for any type of dipping sauce.

Makes 2 cups

2 cups vanilla Greek yogurt, wheat-free
½ cup honey
¼ teaspoon lemon juice
½ teaspoon cinnamon

Corn Dog Muffins

Makes 24 muffins or 48 mini muffins

1 (16-ounce) package of hot dogs (beef, turkey, chicken, or veggie), wheat-free
1 cup all-purpose wheat-free flour
1 cup yellow cornmeal
¼ cup turbinado sugar
2 teaspoons wheat-free baking powder
½ teaspoon salt
1 cup milk or buttermilk
2 eggs
¼ teaspoon wheat-free vanilla extract
¼ cup butter, softened
¼ cup unsweetened applesauce

The whole family will love these. These make a delicious kid-friendly meal or a simple appetizer.

1. Preheat the oven to 425°F. Spray muffin tins with nonstick cooking spray or line with muffin liners.

2. Cut hot dogs into ¼" pieces.

3. In a medium-sized bowl, mix together flour, cornmeal, sugar, baking powder, and salt.

4. Stir in milk, eggs, vanilla, butter, and applesauce, and mix until smooth.

5. Pour chopped hot dogs into corn bread batter. Stir well. Fill ¾ of each muffin tin with corn bread/hotdog batter.

6. Bake until muffins become light brown and center is thoroughly cooked, about 12–15 minutes. Cool for a few minutes before serving.

Additional Goodies

Feel free to add whatever extras you'd like to these corn muffins. Sweet peppers, jalapeño peppers, broccoli, onions, basil, cilantro, and shredded cheese all make wonderful additions.

No Bake Peanut Butter–Flax Bites

These simple bars are an easy after-school snack for children or a quick treat. These are so much healthier than other treats with a long list of ingredients.

1. Stir all ingredients together in a medium-sized bowl until thoroughly mixed. Spread in a 9" × 9" pan and place in the refrigerator to cool.

2. Cut the bites into small squares. Store in an airtight container and keep refrigerated for up to 1 week.

Alternatives

This recipe is so versatile, the possibilities are endless. You can use sunflower seed butter, cashew butter, or almond butter in place of the peanut butter. You can substitute chopped dried cranberries, raisins, cherries, or nuts for the chocolate chips. You can also roll them into little balls instead of cutting them into squares. This is a fun activity kids will enjoy helping with.

Makes 20 bites

1 cup dry old-fashioned wheat-free oats

½ cup dark chocolate chips, wheat-free

½ cup natural peanut butter

½ cup ground flaxseed

⅓ cup honey

1 teaspoon wheat-free vanilla extract

Snacks and Smoothies

Chapter 16

Raspberry Yogurt Smoothie

Serves 2

1 cup plain non-fat Greek yogurt, wheat-free

½ cup frozen raspberries

½ cup fat-free milk (almond, soy, or whatever milk you choose)

½ banana

2 tablespoons ground flaxseed

Smoothies are a wonderful, healthy, and filling alternative to standard breakfast options and they make a nutritious snack any time of day. They are so versatile and can be used with so many different ingredients.

Place all of the ingredients in blender for 1–2 minutes until thoroughly blended. Serve immediately.

The Benefits of Flax

Flax is a seed that is packed with more antioxidants, fiber, and omega-3 fatty acids than just about anything its size. These omega-3 fatty acids are the ones that fight inflammation in the body and help prevent diseases and chronic illnesses. Ground flaxseed can be found in most supermarkets and health food stores.

Chocolate–Peanut Butter Smoothie

This smoothie is so delicious, you won't even believe that it is healthy!

Combine all ingredients in a blender and blend until thick and creamy. Serve immediately.

Looking to Add More Protein to Your Smoothie?

Protein powder is an easy way to increase your protein, especially in smoothies. There are many varieties of protein powders. Read your labels carefully to make sure the protein powders have no ingredients containing wheat.

Serves 2

2 tablespoons unsweetened cocoa powder
2 tablespoons natural creamy peanut butter
½ banana, frozen
½ cup almond milk (or milk of your choice)
½ cup plain Greek low-fat yogurt, wheat-free
½ teaspoon wheat-free vanilla extract
4–5 ice cubes

Blueberry-Oatmeal Smoothie

Serves 2

½ cup wheat-free rolled oats
1 cup soy milk
1 banana, frozen
¾ cup fresh or frozen organic
blueberries
1 teaspoon honey (optional)
4–5 ice cubes (if using fresh
blueberries)

Wheat-free rolled oats add a wonderful texture to your average smoothie.

Place the oats in a blender and blend for 1–2 minutes until they are ground into a fine powder. Add the rest of the ingredients, blend, and enjoy!

Freeze-Ahead Fruit

Frozen fruit is perfect for smoothies and you can always keep it in your freezer. Feel free to mix it up and use whatever fruit you have on hand.

Sneaky Kiwi-Pineapple Smoothie

This smoothie is a terrific way to "sneak" vegetables into your kids' smoothies! If they are suspicious of the bright green color, tell them that it's the kiwi that turned the smoothie green.

Place all the ingredients in a blender. Blend until smooth. Serve immediately.

Makes 2 smoothies

1 cup pineapple chunks, fresh or frozen

2 kiwis, peeled and chopped

½ banana

6 ounces plain Greek yogurt, wheat-free

½ cup pineapple juice

Ice (you can use less if you use frozen pineapple)

2 tablespoons chia or flaxseed (optional)

1 cup spinach or kale (optional)

Mixed Berry Smoothie

Serves 2–3

2 cups unflavored almond milk,
    or milk of your choice
1 tablespoon pure maple syrup
1 teaspoon wheat-free vanilla
    extract
½ cup frozen raspberries
½ cup frozen strawberries
1 tablespoon coconut oil
½ teaspoon cinnamon
½ cup blueberries, frozen

This smoothie is ideal for breakfast or as a snack. You can substitute different frozen fruits if you do not have frozen berries in your house.

1. Place all ingredients into a blender container in the order listed.

2. Blend until smooth, about 1 minute. Pour into glasses and serve.

Quinoa Granola with Dried Cranberries

This granola is the perfect breakfast, snack, or dessert.

1. Preheat the oven to 225°F.

2. In a large bowl, combine the dry ingredients (first 4 ingredients). Add the nuts, seeds, and coconut. Mix well.

3. Stir to combine thoroughly while adding in the cinnamon, ginger, and allspice.

4. Mix in maple syrup, vanilla, melted coconut oil, dates, and cranberries. Make sure everything is evenly distributed and coated well.

5. Spoon and press mixture onto baking sheet lined with wax paper or parchment paper. Bake for 60 minutes.

6. Let cool after removing from oven then pull corners of wax paper together to crumble granola. Store in airtight container when cooled for up to 3 days.

Serves 8

1 cup wheat-free whole rolled oats
1 cup buckwheat groats
⅓ cup uncooked quinoa, rinsed and drained
2 tablespoons ground chia seeds
¾ cup raw chopped pecans
¼ cup raw pumpkin seeds
¼ cup raw sunflower seeds
¼ cup raw chopped walnuts
½ cup shredded coconut, unsweetened
2 teaspoons cinnamon
1 teaspoon ground ginger
1 teaspoon allspice, wheat-free
½ cup real maple syrup
1 tablespoon wheat-free vanilla extract
¼ cup organic coconut oil, melted
⅓ cup chopped dates
⅓ cup dried cranberries, unsweetened, wheat-free

Frozen Chocolate Covered Banana Bites

Makes 30 bites

2 ripe bananas (not too ripe or
  they won't work)
1 cup wheat-free baking
  chocolate
1 tablespoon milk
Toothpicks
Shredded coconut, slivered
  almonds, or toffee bits for
  toppings (optional)

These are the perfectly portioned snack or dessert. Children and adults alike love these little treats.

1. Line a baking sheet with wax or parchment paper.

2. Cut bananas into ½" thick slices and place them on the lined baking sheet. Place them in the freezer on the tray while you melt the chocolate.

3. Place the chocolate in a small saucepan and melt over low heat while stirring continuously. Add milk and continue to stir until completely melted. Remove from heat.

4. Place a toothpick (or you can use a fork) in each banana slice and dip into melted chocolate. Place on lined baking sheet.

5. You can pour some extra melted chocolate on top of banana slices. Sprinkle with shredded coconut, slivered almonds, or whatever topping you like.

6. Transfer tray to freezer for a minimum of 1 hour or until completely frozen. Store in an airtight container in the freezer.

Cranberry-Apple Granola Cookie Bars

These bars are like a cookie and a granola bar in one. There is no need to buy the store-bought granola bars anymore. These are healthy and delicious.

1. Preheat the oven to 350°F.

2. In a large bowl, mix the oats, walnuts, flax, almond meal, coconut, and salt. Place on baking sheet and roast in the oven for 15 minutes, stirring occasionally.

3. Dissolve honey and vanilla in saucepan over low heat.

4. Remove dry ingredients from the oven and pour into a bowl. Lower oven to 300°F. Grease a 9" × 13" glass dish with cooking spray.

5. Mix honey mixture into bowl with dry ingredients; add the cranberries and apples.

6. Pour into greased dish and spread out evenly. Use rubber spatula to press down evenly. Bake for 30–40 minutes, until golden brown.

7. Let cool for at least 1½–2 hours to harden.

Makes 25 bars

3 cups wheat-free rolled oats
¾ cup walnuts, finely chopped
¾ cup ground flaxseed
⅓ cup almond meal
½ cup shredded coconut
⅛ teaspoon kosher salt
1¼ cups honey
1 teaspoon wheat-free vanilla extract
2 ounces dried cranberries, unsweetened, wheat-free
2 ounces dried apple slices, unsweetened, wheat-free

Green Tea–Kiwi Popsicles

Makes 4 popsicles

1½ teaspoons green tea matcha powder

1 tablespoon boiling water

2 kiwis, peeled and diced

12 ounces vanilla Greek yogurt, wheat-free

1 teaspoon fresh lemon juice

3 tablespoons honey

These are healthy and refreshing. If you are making these for children you can easily use decaffeinated green tea matcha powder.

1. In a small bowl, combine matcha powder and boiling water. Stir to combine to create a smooth paste. Set aside.

2. In a large bowl, mix the diced kiwis, Greek yogurt, lemon juice, and honey. Stir in matcha paste, and make sure it is thoroughly combined.

3. Spoon mixture into popsicle molds, making sure to only fill ¾ of the way. Place in the freezer until frozen.

Blueberry Frozen Yogurt

This wonderful, light snack can be made with any berries you have on hand. You can also use frozen berries and defrost them before you mix with the yogurt.

1. In a medium bowl, mix the milk and sugar until the sugar is dissolved, about 1–2 minutes on low speed.

2. Stir in the yogurt and strawberry purée.

3. In an ice cream maker, freeze according to manufacturer's instructions. You can spoon the frozen yogurt into a tall, upright plastic container to place in the freezer for up to a week.

Simply Homemade

Store-bought frozen yogurt and ice cream can have over twenty ingredients in them! This recipe is a perfect example of how easy it is to make your own frozen yogurt at home with only 4 ingredients and ensure it is wheat-free.

Serves 14

¾ cup milk
¼ cup turbinado sugar
4 cups vanilla Greek yogurt, wheat-free
2 cups strawberries, puréed

Homemade Sweet Potato Chips

Makes about 3 dozen chips

2 large sweet potatoes, peeled
3 cups canola oil
Salt and pepper, to taste
1 teaspoon cinnamon (optional)

Sweet potatoes are loaded with vitamin A and are very delicious when fried and salted. (You can substitute plantains for a taste of the islands.)

1. Slice the potatoes thinly with a mandoline.

2. Heat the oil in a deep-fat fryer to 375°F.

3. Fry potato slices for about 3–4 minutes, depending on the thickness of the chips. When the chips are very crisp, remove from the oil and drain.

4. Add salt, pepper, and cinnamon if desired. Serve with dip or eat plain.

Veggie-Chips!
These "chips" can be prepared with a variety of different vegetables. You can make eggplant, zucchini, or even parsnip chips. The kids won't even suspect they are healthy!

Parmesan-Kale Chips

Low calorie and nutritious, these make the perfect snack for the little ones. Just like potato chips, you can eat the whole bowl in one sitting.

1. Preheat an oven to 350°F. Line a non-insulated cookie sheet with parchment paper.

2. With a knife or kitchen shears, carefully remove the kale leaves from the thick stems and tear into bite-sized pieces. Wash and thoroughly dry kale with a salad spinner.

3. Spray the kale with olive oil from Misto sprayer and sprinkle with salt and Parmesan.

4. Bake until the edges brown, but are not burnt, 10–15 minutes.

Serves 6

1 bunch kale (the curly kind is less bitter)
1 tablespoon extra-virgin olive oil in Misto sprayer
1 teaspoon salt
1 tablespoon finely and freshly grated Parmesan cheese

Brown Rice Chips

Serves 8

1 package of brown rice tortillas, wheat-free

1 tablespoon cinnamon

1 tablespoon turbinado sugar

½ teaspoon cloves

½ teaspoon allspice, wheat-free

These chips will be a favorite in your house. They will stay fresh in an airtight container for up to a week.

1. Preheat the oven to 350°F. Cut the tortillas into slices.

2. In a small bowl combine the cinnamon, sugar, and spices together.

3. Lay tortilla slices out in a single layer on a baking sheet and sprinkle with cinnamon spice/sugar mixture.

4. Bake 8–12 minutes, until chips start to lightly brown. Repeat with remaining tortilla slices. Let cool 10 minutes and serve with chilled Tropical Fruit Salsa (see Chapter 15).

Roasted Pink Pepper Nuts

These will keep for up to one week in a tight plastic or tin container. You can also substitute black or white pepper with only slightly different results.

1. Preheat the oven to 350°F. Line a cookie sheet with aluminum foil and treat with non-stick spray.

2. In a saucepan over medium heat, melt the butter, add sugar and water, and mix well.

3. Add the spices, salt, and peppercorns. When well blended, add the almonds and coat.

4. Transfer the nuts to the cookie sheet. Bake for about 10 minutes, until well browned. Cool and store in airtight container.

Makes 2½ cups

½ stick (¼ cup) unsalted butter
¾ cup golden brown sugar (not "Brownulated")
4 teaspoons water
½ teaspoon ground cloves
⅛ teaspoon ground nutmeg
¼ teaspoon cinnamon
2 teaspoons salt
1 tablespoon freshly ground pink peppercorns
2½ cups blanched almonds

Strawberry-Vanilla Cheesecake with Walnut Crust

Raspberry-Blueberry Coulis

Orange-Carrot Cake

Crispy Chocolate-Mint Meringue Cookies

Apple Cobbler

Peanut Butter Cookies

Chestnut Cookies

Pavlova with Chocolate and Bananas

Apple Brown Betty with Corn Bread

Lemon Clouds

Naturally Red Velvet Cupcakes with Cream Cheese Frosting

Cream Cheese Frosting

Pumpkin Pie with Pecan Crust

Pecan Crust

Chocolate Mousse

Pumpkin Custard

Rice Pudding

Desserts and Goodies

Chapter 17

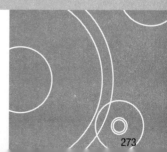

Strawberry-Vanilla Cheesecake with Walnut Crust

Serves 10–12

1½ cups ground walnuts
½ cup sugar
½ teaspoon cinnamon, ground
½ cup unsalted butter, melted
4 eggs, separated
3 (8-ounce) packages cream cheese
1 cup sour cream, wheat-free
2 teaspoons wheat-free vanilla extract
1 teaspoon salt
2 tablespoons rice flour
⅔ cup strawberry preserves, melted

This is a fine combination with a delightful flavor and smooth consistency.

1. Mix together the walnuts, sugar, cinnamon, and melted butter. Prepare a springform pan with nonstick spray and press the nut mixture into the bottom to form a crust. Chill for at least 1 hour.

2. Preheat the oven to 350°F.

3. Beat the egg whites and set aside.

4. In a large bowl, using an electric mixer, beat the cream cheese, sour cream, vanilla, salt, and rice flour together.

5. Add the egg yolks, one at a time, while beating. When smooth, fold in the egg whites and mix in the strawberry preserves.

6. Pour into the springform pan and bake for 1 hour. Turn off oven and crack the door. Let cake cool for another hour. Chill before serving.

Nut Crusts for Cheesecake

This recipe specifies walnuts because they are probably the least expensive shelled nut and work well in these recipes. However, you can substitute hazelnuts, almonds, or pecans. Pecans add a Southern touch and are really good (see the Pumpkin Pie with Pecan Crust recipe in this chapter). Grinding nuts is simple—just use your food processor.

Raspberry-Blueberry Coulis

This is wonderful not only on crepes but on wheat-free ice cream and pancakes as well. You can also mix it into Rice Pudding (see recipe in this chapter) for a different take on an old-fashioned dessert.

Place all of the ingredients in a saucepan and bring to a boil. Remove from heat and cool. Whisk until smooth. Serve warm or cool.

Makes 1½ cups

½ pint fresh blueberries, rinsed
½ pint fresh raspberries, rinsed
¼ cup water
¼ cup sugar
1" × ½" strip orange rind

Orange-Carrot Cake

Serves 8–10

4 eggs, separated
½ cup brown sugar
1½ cups grated carrots
1 tablespoon lemon juice
Grated rind of ½ fresh orange
½ cup corn flour
1"-piece fresh gingerroot, peeled and minced
1 teaspoon cinnamon
1½ teaspoons baking soda
½ teaspoon salt

This delicious cake has a nice zing with the addition of a little lemon juice and the grated orange rind. The gingerroot adds an appealing sophistication.

1. Liberally butter a springform pan and preheat the oven to 325°F.

2. Beat the egg whites until stiff and set aside.

3. Beat the egg yolks, sugar, and carrots together. Add the lemon juice, orange rind, and corn flour. Mix until smooth, then add the gingerroot, cinnamon, baking soda, and salt. Gently fold in the egg whites.

4. Pour the cake batter into the springform pan and bake for 1 hour. Test by plunging a toothpick into the center of the cake—if the pick comes out clean, the cake is done.

What's Up, Doc?

Carrot cake was created during World War II when flour and sugar were rationed. The sweetness of carrots contributed to this cake, and when oranges were available, it became a feast. Cooks used their fuel carefully too, baking and making stews and soups in the oven all at the same time. Sometimes, hard times make for sweet endings.

Crispy Chocolate-Mint Meringue Cookies

These are crisp and delicious. The nuts add a wonderful crunch. Use either blanched almonds or hazelnuts.

1. Preheat the oven to 275°F. Line two cookie sheets with parchment paper.

2. Sift ¼ cup of sugar and ¼ cup of cocoa together in a bowl. Add salt.

3. In a separate bowl, beat egg whites, mint extract, and cream of tartar. When peaks begin to form, add the remaining ¼ cup sugar, a teaspoon at a time. Slowly beat in the cocoa mixture. The meringue should be stiff and shiny.

4. Add chopped nuts. Drop by teaspoonfuls on the parchment paper. Bake for 45–50 minutes. Cool on baking sheets. You can place these in an airtight cookie tin or serve them the same day.

Ugly, But Good!

These cookies are known in Italy as "ugly but good"! Other, kinder descriptions include "kisses" and "crisps." They are a bit dumpy looking, but just try one. This recipe is a simplification of the original, far more time-consuming one.

Makes about 40 cookies

½ cup sugar, divided

¼ cup unsweetened cocoa powder

⅛ teaspoon salt

3 egg whites (from extra-large eggs)

⅛ teaspoon peppermint extract

⅛ teaspoon cream of tartar

½ cup hazelnuts, lightly toasted, skinned, and coarsely chopped

Apple Cobbler

Serves 10

8 large tart apples such as
   Granny Smiths, peeled,
   cored, and sliced
½ cup fresh lemon juice
1 teaspoon cinnamon, ground
1 cup sugar, divided
1 stick (½ cup) unsalted butter,
   melted
½ teaspoon salt
1½ cups rice flour or quinoa
   flour
1 tablespoon wheat-free baking
   powder
1 cup buttermilk

This smells like autumn but tastes wonderful
any time of the year.

1. Preheat the oven to 375°F.

2. Place apples into a bowl and sprinkle with
lemon juice, cinnamon, and ½ cup sugar. Mix
well.

3. Prepare a 9" × 13" baking dish with nonstick spray. Spread the apples on the bottom.

4. Pour the melted butter into a large bowl.
Add the remaining ½ cup sugar and salt, and
whisk in the flour and baking powder. Add the
buttermilk and stir; don't worry about lumps.

5. Drop the batter by tablespoonfuls over the
fruit. Bake for 35–40 minutes. Cool for 25 minutes. Serve with wheat-free vanilla ice cream or
whipped cream.

Peanut Butter Cookies

These are quite addicting, you might find it difficult to eat just one! These are equally as delicious with or without chocolate chips.

1. Preheat the oven to 350°F.

2. In a medium-sized mixing bowl, combine the peanut butter, sugars, egg, vanilla, and baking soda. Mix thoroughly. Add chocolate chips and diced nuts if desired.

3. Line a baking sheet with parchment paper. Spoon cookie dough by tablespoonfuls onto baking sheet. Bake for 12–15 minutes, until centers are cooked and edges are lightly browned. Let them cool on the sheet for 5–10 minutes before transferring to a wire rack to cool completely.

Makes 2–3 dozen cookies, depending on size

1 cup natural peanut butter, well stirred

½ cup turbinado sugar

⅓ cup brown sugar

1 large egg, beaten

½ teaspoon wheat-free vanilla extract

½ teaspoon baking soda

1 cup wheat-free chocolate chips (optional)

½ cup almonds or nut of your choice, finely diced

Chestnut Cookies

Makes about 48 cookies

1 (2-ounce) can chestnuts, roasted, peeled, and packed in water

1½ cups chestnut flour

½ cup milk

2 egg yolks

1 teaspoon wheat-free vanilla extract

½ teaspoon nutmeg

1 teaspoon salt

2 teaspoons wheat-free baking powder

½ cup granulated sugar

½ cup unsalted butter, melted

3 egg whites, beaten stiff

These cookies are delicious around the holidays. They are so unique and delightful the whole family will love them.

1. Preheat the oven to 350°F.

2. Drain the chestnuts and chop in the food processor. Place in the bowl of an electric mixer. With the motor on low, add the chestnut flour, milk, egg yolks, vanilla, nutmeg, salt, baking powder, sugar, and melted butter.

3. Fold the egg whites into the chestnut mixture. Drop by the teaspoonful on cookie sheets lined with parchment paper.

4. Bake for 12–15 minutes. Cool and place on platters for immediate use, or store in tins for later use.

Chestnuts—Raw, Jarred, or Canned?

Preparing chestnuts can be a real pain! You have to make cross slits in each, then either boil or roast them, and get the shells off. Then, you have to peel off the skins. This process is time consuming. However, you can buy prepared chestnuts in jars and cans and avoid all that work. Of course, your house won't smell like roasted chestnuts, but you'll have more time to enjoy them.

Pavlova with Chocolate and Bananas

Pavlova is a meringue dessert cake with a whipped cream topping. Place the whipped cream on the pavlova right before serving as it will become soft and doesn't usually hold for more than a few hours.

1. Preheat the oven to 200°F.

2. Whip the egg whites, and as they stiffen, add the vinegar and vanilla extract and slowly add the ½ cup sugar. Pour into a 9" glass pie pan that you've treated with nonstick spray.

3. Bake the meringue for 2 hours. Then, turn off the oven and crack the door. Let the meringue rest for another hour. It should become very crisp and lightly browned. Do not prepare ahead of time if the weather is humid.

4. Melt the chocolate, butter, and sugar. Cool until it's still liquid but room temperature.

5. Peel and slice 1 banana in single layer into the meringue crust. Spoon half of the chocolate sauce over banana slices. Slice the other banana into another layer over chocolate sauce, then spoon the remaining sauce on top of bananas, and top with whipped cream.

Blanching

When you blanch a peach, a tomato, or a nectarine, you plunge it into boiling water for a minute. You don't cook it, you just loosen the skin. If you are blanching a great many pieces, have a colander next to your pot of boiling water and a pot of ice water in the sink. Use a slotted spoon to remove the fruit from the boiling water, put it into the colander, and then plunge it into the ice water. After it is cool enough to handle, slip off the skin and cut it up.

Serves 6

4 egg whites
1 teaspoon vinegar, wheat-free
½ teaspoon wheat-free vanilla extract
½ cup sugar
3 squares semisweet chocolate, wheat-free
½ cup unsalted butter
⅓ cup sugar
2 bananas, kept in the freezer for 20 minutes to firm
1 cup heavy cream, whipped with 2 teaspoons wheat-free confectioners' sugar

Apple Brown Betty with Corn Bread

Serves 4

4 large tart apples, peeled, cored, and sliced

Juice of ½ lemon

2 cups wheat-free corn bread cubes

2 eggs, lightly beaten

1½ cups milk

1 teaspoon wheat-free vanilla extract

¼ teaspoon ground nutmeg

¼ teaspoon ginger

1 teaspoon ground cinnamon

⅛ teaspoon ground cloves

½ teaspoon salt

½ cup dark brown sugar, or to taste

½ cup butter

Now you know what to do with old, stale bread. You can make it into a delicious, homey baked pudding.

1. Preheat the oven to 350°F. Liberally butter a 2-quart casserole dish or treat it with nonstick spray.

2. Put the apples in the casserole and sprinkle with lemon juice. Add the bread cubes. Mix well.

3. Beat together the eggs, milk, vanilla, spices, salt, and sugar. Mix with the apples and bread cubes. Dot with butter.

4. Bake for 45 minutes, or until brown on top and very moist inside. Serve warm with whipped cream or ice cream.

Why Not Use Canned Whipped Cream?

Whipped cream that comes in aerosol spray cans is much sweeter than the cream you would whip yourself. Also, there is more air than cream, so you are paying a premium for the spray convenience. When you do your own cream whipping, you will get a lot more flavor, no additives, and a healthier end product.

Lemon Clouds

Light and delicious—this is a delight, any time of year.

1. In the container of a blender, sprinkle the gelatin over the water. Let rest for 4–5 minutes.

2. Add the lemon juice, lemon rind, vanilla, sugar, boiling water, and butter. Blend until well mixed. Cool.

3. Beat the egg whites until stiff. Fold them into the lemon mixture. Chill in the refrigerator, stirring every half hour. Place in individual glasses or bowls. Serve with lots of fresh berries.

Serves 4–6

1½ teaspoons unflavored gelatin
2 tablespoons cool water
Juice of 1 fresh lemon
1 tablespoon minced lemon rind
½ teaspoon wheat-free vanilla extract
½ cup sugar, or to taste
1 cup boiling water
2 tablespoons unsalted butter
4 egg whites

Naturally Red Velvet Cupcakes with Cream Cheese Frosting

Makes 12 cupcakes

1¼ cups wheat-free, all-purpose flour

½ teaspoon, plus ⅛ teaspoon, xanthan gum

¾ cup turbinado sugar

2 tablespoons cocoa powder, unsweetened

1 teaspoon wheat-free baking powder

¼ teaspoon salt

6 beets, steamed

¼ cup 100% maple syrup

⅓ cup unsweetened applesauce

2 tablespoons lemon juice (juice from about 1 large lemon)

1½ teaspoons wheat-free vanilla extract

Cream Cheese Frosting (see recipe in this chapter)

There is no need for artificial colors in these cupcakes. Beets make these cupcakes a wonderful red color.

1. Preheat the oven to 350°F. Line 12 cupcake tins with liners.

2. In a large bowl, whisk together the flour, xanthan gum, sugar, cocoa, baking powder, and salt so that all of the ingredients are evenly dispersed throughout the mixture. Set aside.

3. Pour the beets into your food processor or blender, slow adding small amounts of water if it becomes too thick. Process the beets for a solid 2–4 minutes, depending on how powerful your machine is, until completely smooth.

4. Add the maple syrup, applesauce, lemon juice, and vanilla, and pulse briefly to incorporate. If you are not using a high-efficiency blender, add 1 tablespoon of water at a time if mixture is too thick.

5. Pour the beet mixture into the bowl of dry ingredients, and mix just enough to combine.

6. Equally distribute the batter between your prepared tins, and bake for 18–22 minutes, until a toothpick inserted into the center comes out clean. Let cool completely before frosting with Cream Cheese Frosting.

Cream Cheese Frosting

This frosting can be a wonderful topping for any cake or cookie. Unlike the store-bought varieties, this simple frosting only has 4 ingredients.

1. In a large mixing bowl, mix the butter, cream cheese, and vanilla until smooth with a hand-held blender.

2. Add the powdered sugar and beat until smooth.

3. Store any frosting in airtight container in the refrigerator for 3–5 days.

Makes frosting for 15–18 cupcakes

2 tablespoons unsalted butter, softened

3 ounces cream cheese, softened

½ teaspoon wheat-free vanilla extract

1 cup powdered sugar, wheat-free

Pumpkin Pie with Pecan Crust

Serves 8

15 ounces pumpkin

¾ cup milk

¾ cup 100% maple syrup

3 egg whites

2 teaspoons cinnamon

1 teaspoon pumpkin pie spice, wheat-free

1 Pecan Crust (see recipe in this chapter)

This pie is a perfect dessert any time of year, not just during the holidays. You can use non-fat milk in this recipe to lighten it up, and it will still taste delicious.

1. Preheat the oven to 350°F.

2. Mix all the ingredients together in a medium-sized mixing bowl until well combined.

3. Pour batter into prepared pecan crust. Bake about 55–60 minutes, or until a toothpick inserted into the center comes out clean.

Pecan Crust

Anyone eating this pie crust will not believe this is made with pecans. So simple and tasty, and wheat-free.

1. Preheat the oven to 350°F.

2. Place the pecans in a food processor and process until you have a coarse flour.

3. Add the almond flour, salt, baking soda, cinnamon, pumpkin pie spice, vanilla, coconut oil, maple syrup, and egg, and pulse until a ball of dough forms.

4. Using the palms of your hands, press the dough into the bottom and up the sides of a pie pan. Spread into a thin layer throughout the sides and bottom. Bake for 10 minutes.

Serves 8

¾ cup pecans
1 cup blanched almond flour
⅛ teaspoon salt
¼ teaspoon baking soda
½ teaspoon cinnamon
½ teaspoon wheat-free pumpkin pie spice (cinnamon, ginger, allspice, and nutmeg)
1 teaspoon wheat-free vanilla extract
4 tablespoons coconut oil (or cold butter)
3 tablespoons 100% maple syrup
1 egg

Chocolate Mousse

Serves 6–8

4 squares semisweet chocolate, wheat-free

¼ cup rum or cognac

½ cup sugar, or to taste

1 teaspoon instant coffee powder

¼ cup boiling water

5 eggs, separated

1 cup heavy cream, whipped stiff with 1 tablespoon sugar

The classic darling of the French bistro, this is a fresh take on an old favorite. If you'd like to lighten it up, substitute half-and-half for the heavy cream.

1. Combine the chocolate, rum or cognac, and sugar in a heavy saucepan or the top of a double boiler.

2. Mix the coffee powder with boiling water and add to the chocolate mixture.

3. Cook over very low heat, stirring from time to time, until the chocolate melts. Remove from the heat and cool for 3 minutes.

4. Slowly beat in the egg yolks, one at a time.

5. Let cool and fold in the egg whites. Spoon into a serving bowl or dessert glasses. Chill for 4–6 hours. Serve with homemade whipped cream.

Garnishes for Chocolate Mousse

Fresh raspberries are perfect garnishes for chocolate mousse, as are sprigs of mint. You can also pour a bit of peppermint schnapps over each serving for an added kick. Chambord, a black raspberry liqueur, would also be a wonderful substitution for rum or cognac when added to the mousse when you are making it.

Pumpkin Custard

You can substitute frozen winter (butternut) squash for the pumpkin with good results. If you do use canned pumpkin, make sure the label says 100 percent pumpkin, not pumpkin pie filling.

1. Preheat the oven to 325°F.

2. Purée the pumpkin in your blender or food processor. Slowly add the rest of the ingredients.

3. Pour into a buttered casserole dish. Place a roasting pan of hot water in the middle of the oven. Put the bowl of pumpkin custard in the roasting pan and bake for 50–60 minutes. A nice variation is to add a cup of pecan pieces and let them bake right into the custard.

Serves 6–8

2 cups cubed fresh pumpkin, steamed in 1 cup water, or 2 (12–13 ounce) packages frozen winter squash, thawed
½ cup brown sugar
¼ cup white sugar
½ teaspoon each: ground ginger, ground cloves, ground nutmeg
1 teaspoon ground cinnamon
3 eggs, beaten
1 cup heavy cream

Rice Pudding

Serves 6

1 tablespoon butter
1½ cups water
¾ cup arborio rice, uncooked
1 egg
2 cups milk, divided
⅓ cup turbinado sugar
¼ teaspoon salt
½ cup golden raisins
1 teaspoon cinnamon
½ teaspoon nutmeg
½ teaspoon wheat-free vanilla
   extract

This classic dessert is an extremely popular dessert in many restaurants. You can save some calories and fat by using reduced fat milk and cutting back on the sugar to ¼ cup.

1. Melt the butter in a medium saucepan. Add 1½ cups water and bring to boil. Stir rice into boiling water. Reduce heat to low, cover, and simmer about 20 minutes, until all water has been absorbed.

2. Place the egg in a small bowl and beat. Slowly add ½ cup of milk to the egg. Set aside.

3. Add 1½ cups milk, sugar, and salt to the cooked rice. Cook over medium heat about 30 minutes, until it begins to get thicker and creamier.

4. Slowly add in egg/milk mixture making sure to stir constantly.

5. Add raisins, cinnamon, nutmeg, and vanilla. Continue to cook another 2 minutes, while stirring constantly. Serve warm or cold.

Temper, Temper

What does it mean to "temper an egg"? It simply means to slowly add the beaten egg to the hot milk while stirring. If you just dump the egg mixture in, you could end up with scrambled eggs in the mixture, which wouldn't be tasty in a rice pudding.

Resources

Appendix

http://wheat-free.org

www.foodallergygourmet.com

www.foodallergens.info/Allergenic_Foods/Allergy_Foods.html

http://gluten.lovetoknow.com/List_of_Wheat_Free_Foods

www.webmd.com/allergies/guide/wheat-allergy

www.foodallergy.org/home

http://foodallergies.about.com/od/wheatallergies/a/Wheat-Allergy.htm

www.glutenfree.com

www.glutenfreeliving.com

www.celiac.com

http://celiacdisease.about.com/od/glutenfreefoodshoppin1/ss/Gluten-Free-Food-List.htm

Standard U.S./
Metric Measurement Conversions

VOLUME CONVERSIONS

U.S. Volume Measure	Metric Equivalent
⅛ teaspoon	0.5 milliliter
¼ teaspoon	1 milliliter
½ teaspoon	2 milliliters
1 teaspoon	5 milliliters
½ tablespoon	7 milliliters
1 tablespoon (3 teaspoons)	15 milliliters
2 tablespoons (1 fluid ounce)	30 milliliters
¼ cup (4 tablespoons)	60 milliliters
⅓ cup	90 milliliters
½ cup (4 fluid ounces)	125 milliliters
⅔ cup	160 milliliters
¾ cup (6 fluid ounces)	180 milliliters
1 cup (16 tablespoons)	250 milliliters
1 pint (2 cups)	500 milliliters
1 quart (4 cups)	1 liter (about)

WEIGHT CONVERSIONS

U.S. Weight Measure	Metric Equivalent
½ ounce	15 grams
1 ounce	30 grams
2 ounces	60 grams
3 ounces	85 grams
¼ pound (4 ounces)	115 grams
½ pound (8 ounces)	225 grams
¾ pound (12 ounces)	340 grams
1 pound (16 ounces)	454 grams

OVEN TEMPERATURE CONVERSIONS

Degrees Fahrenheit	Degrees Celsius
200 degrees F	95 degrees C
250 degrees F	120 degrees C
275 degrees F	135 degrees C
300 degrees F	150 degrees C
325 degrees F	160 degrees C
350 degrees F	180 degrees C
375 degrees F	190 degrees C
400 degrees F	205 degrees C
425 degrees F	220 degrees C
450 degrees F	230 degrees C

BAKING PAN SIZES

U.S.	Metric
8 × 1½ inch round baking pan	20 × 4 cm cake tin
9 × 1½ inch round baking pan	23 × 3.5 cm cake tin
11 × 7 × 1½ inch baking pan	28 × 18 × 4 cm baking tin
13 × 9 × 2 inch baking pan	30 × 20 × 5 cm baking tin
2 quart rectangular baking dish	30 × 20 × 3 cm baking tin
15 × 10 × 2 inch baking pan	30 × 25 × 2 cm baking tin (Swiss roll tin)
9 inch pie plate	22 × 4 or 23 × 4 cm pie plate
7 or 8 inch springform pan	18 or 20 cm springform or loose bottom cake tin
9 × 5 × 3 inch loaf pan	23 × 13 × 7 cm or 2 lb narrow loaf or pâté tin
1½ quart casserole	1.5 liter casserole
2 quart casserole	2 liter casserole

Index